Paul,

May the amazing [...]
of God's HOPE arise
in you and through you
more and more!

Forever grateful!

Jeff Cole

What Others Are Saying About Jeff Caliguire and This Book

"For everyone who's wanted to live a powerful life, one filled with meaning, energy and purpose, this book offers you the way to go. It's a terrific resource and a fantastic treasure!"

— Patrick Snow, Publishing Coaching and International Best-Selling Author of *Creating Your Own Destiny*

"*The Habits of Hope: Self Leadership Strategies to Unleash Your Bigger Purpose* is a fantastic read. Caliguire not only has great wisdom to share, but his storytelling is quite engaging. We are often told to have hope, but few have ever ventured to explain how to hope. Caliguire has succeeded at doing that in a very whimsical way. He has great insight into the human struggle for purpose and many practical approaches to help people discover God's will for their lives. Everyone can gain something from this book."

— Moe Girkins, Former CEO of Zondervan Publishing

"Reading through *The Habits of Hope*, my mind began racing with the names of friends and family I want to give this book to. Jeff Caliguire has returned from his own journey to hope to become our guide and he's marked the path for us with twelve powerful, life-changing habits. May the whole world hear!"

— Angela Thomas Pharr, Best-Selling Author & Speaker

"A good story puts you in a setting you've never been before, and once you are there, you find yourself in the story. Jeff Caliguire has done a masterful job taking us to a little place called Hope. Through compelling narrative and enchanted storytelling, the protagonist's quest becomes our quest...his search, our search...his answers, our solutions to life's biggest questions. You will thoroughly enjoy this book."

— Eric Swanson, Leadership Network, Co-author of *The Externally Focused Church* and *To Transform a City*

"Jeff Caliguire has been a continued source of encouragement and hope to me since our time together as student athletes at Cornell University. In his book, *The Habits of Hope,* Jeff shares a powerful story, illustrations, and truths about hope that will bless all who dare to read and embrace the journey."

— Francis X. (Frank) Kelly III, CEO, Kelly & Associates Insurance Group, KELLY Payroll and other KELLY companies, Co-Founder, FCA Lacrosse

"Set in the Adirondacks, this curiously illuminating, genuinely inspiring, and sensitive book gives you the courage and will to survive—in bite-size pieces. Jeff Calguire's philosophy is powerful yet simple as it reveals the power and strength of hope."

— Susan Friedmann, CSP, International Bestselling Author of *Riches in Niches: How to Make it BIG in a small Market*

"When it comes to *The Habits of Hope*, Jeff Caliguire is a man who knows what he's talking about. He has lost hope, found it, figured out how to keep it, and then learned how to guide others into it. All of this is found in his spiritual parable of life and leadership. The book lives up to its billing as a parable, a story of how one man got off the treadmill of existence and into the pilgrimage of purpose. This work is exactly what the title says it is: a book about the life habits that bring hope into our lives, not a book about steps that guarantee results—no such guarantees can ever be given in life. Instead, Jeff offers his readers choices and disciplines that grow hope in our hearts. If you are a reader who wants to make these choices and grow in the disciplines, this book will guide you into a new level of freedom and fruitfulness."

— Dr. William Lawrence, President of Leader Formation,
Senior Professor Emeritus of Pastoral Ministries,
Dallas Theological Seminary, and Author of *Wilderness
Wanderings: Learning to Live the Zigzag Life*

"If you feel like no matter what you do, life isn't going your way, then it's time to take a new look at your thoughts and actions. In this enjoyable parable, Jeff Caliguire takes readers on an adventurous and mystical ride as one man learns how to develop the Habits of Hope that we all need to develop if we wish to live our lives to their fullest potential. Pick it up this book and begin the transformation that will carry you through to the rest of your life!"

— Tyler R. Tichelaar, Ph.D. and Award-Winning Author of
Narrow Lives and *The Best Place*

"Jeff Caliguire has helped countless others, including myself, see qualities in us that we don't always see ourselves. He has also helped us find our God-given purpose and match it up with our profession. Everyone needs direction to get through this crazy life and, now, in this book Jeff nails the habits we need to maintain hope as we wander around. I have enjoyed every book Jeff has written, but this one is his best!"

— Randy Whitaker, Professional Health and Wellness Coach

"Wow! This book is wonderful! I already have two pages of notes for me and my business! In this engaging story, let Jeff Caliguire take you to the beautiful Adirondack Mountains on a crisp, colorful day in October, and through a dangerous canoe trip, to teach the Habits of Hope and change your thinking about life."

— Diane Overgard Founder and President, 45 Degrees

"Hope is the one ingredient human beings can't survive without. The *Habits of Hope* inspired me to, once again, find a fresh stream of hope in my own journey and pass it along to others. Caliguire does a masterful job of telling a story that packs a message ever person needs to hear."

— Jim Candy, Pastor, Ascent Community Church,
Author of *Can I Ask That*

"*The Habits of Hope* will inspire you to move past your own perceived limitations. A relatable story of a man just like you and me, who, through the grace of God, can find passion and purpose in life again. This book brings a refreshment to my spirit and a motivation to redefine personal success as living a faith-filled life of meaningful significance."

—Ron Gelok III, President, Christ Centered Coaching

"This compelling parable offers inspiration and practical tips for anyone wanting a jumpstart on their own journey of discovering (or rediscovering) meaning, purpose, and most of all, hope, in life."

—Jean Blackmer, Author, *MomSense: A Common-Sense Guide to Confident Mothering*

"You owe it to yourself to read this book. Do it today and begin to experience your real life...the one you're meant to live. The habits of hope you'll discover in this story will transform how you think and how you live. The story rings true and the habits really work because Jeff has lived them and has helped countless others, including me, experience them as well. A trip to Hope and the new life it'll bring are waiting for you."

— Gregg Stutts, Marriage Coach and Author of *The Lakeside Conspiracy* and *I Believe God*

"Life is so much more than our present circumstances. This book provides you with tangible ways to find your truth, rise above life's challenges, and successfully lead others."

— Nicole Gabriel, Author of *Finding Your Inner Truth*

"Staring longingly at a mountain wondering what it's like at the peak is completely different from finding a safe pathway and hiking one faith-filled step at a time toward the precipice. Jeff Caliguire has done both, and has earned the right to walk alongside those who fear the journey ahead. *The Habits of Hope* will help you see that there's gold in them there hills…for you!"

— Stephen A. Macchia, Founder and President of Leadership Transformations and author of ten books, including *Becoming a Healthy Church*, *Crafting a Rule of Life*, and *Broken and Whole*

"This book is a must read for anyone who realizes their life now lacks the passion and meaning it once had. Many of us have enjoyed success and found it pretty empty and meaningless; others simply have grown tired of 'putting in the hours' to draw a paycheck. Jeff's book speaks to both groups and provides the tools to break through these doldrums and return to a meaningful life that can make a difference once again. If you are looking for ways to redefine your life from successful to significant, this is the book for you."

— Tom Okarma, President, Vantage Point

"A fun and valuable read! Jeff Caliguire has created a book reminding us that the spirit of hope empowers the leadership of self. Using a fictional but very relatable story, we learn one habit after the next through the journey of Gus and Mr. Turnquest. It's not hard to see our own lives through them, and the practical habits covered in this wonderful book are valuable both individually and collectively."

— Chuck Proudfit, President, At Work On Purpose

"Jeff Caliguire has artfully created a book that can empower us to practically kill our fears and launch our dreams. My guess is it will become a well-worn and highlighted treasure for all who read it."

— Mac Lake, Senior Director, NAMB

A SPIRITUAL PARABLE OF LIFE AND LEADERSHIP

The
HABITS
OF HOPE

SELF-LEADERSHIP STRATEGIES TO UNLEASH
YOUR BIGGER PURPOSE

JEFF CALIGUIRE

AVIVA
PUBLISHING
New York

Address all inquiries to:
Jeff.Caliguire@ConvergencePoint.Biz
www.TheHabitsofHope.com

ISBN: 978-1-943164-87-5 (hardcover)
978-1-943164-88-2 (ebook)
Library of Congress #: 2016950040

Editors: Tyler Tichelaar & Larry Alexander, Superior Book Productions
Cover and Interior Design: Nicole Gabriel, AngelDog Productions

Published by:
Aviva Publishing
Lake Placid, NY
(518)523-1320
www.avivapubs.com

Every attempt has been made to source properly all quotes.

Printed in the USA
First Edition

For additional copies visit:
www.TheHabitsofHope.com or e-mail Jeff.Caliguire@ConvergencePoint.Biz

DEDICATION

To those who believe in, mentor, and coach youth of all ages. You likely have no earthly idea the way you've influenced and shaped us when you thought we didn't care or notice. You're the ones who've brought us back from the abyss of despair and planted us safely in the land of Hope. You've been role models, heroes, and in some cases, parents to us.

You believed in us when we couldn't *yet* believe in ourselves. You walked the talk, often without hearing or receiving the praise you so deserved. You are the salt of the earth and the light of the world!

In my own case, this book is lovingly dedicated to those who inspired me to tell this story (some of whom have already graduated from it!).

My family: Mindy Caliguire, Jeff M. Caliguire, Jon Caliguire, Josh Caliguire.

Robert and Gloria Caliguire (Mom and Dad. They saw something in me and in this book and cheered it all the way to the finish!)

Mike and Peg McGarry (My other Mom and Dad, who call me their "son-in-love"!)

Those who prayed for me every single day when I was a kid (which still blows me away!): Henry Spellmeyer, Dena Mortland,

Ethel Meroni, Mary Caliguiri, Ed Young, and Harold Buirkle.

And to my mentors and coaches, whom I will love forever: Paul Feeney, Pete Nelson, Rick Holladay, Chuck Tompkins, Bill and Margaret Wheeler, Jim Rumsey, Joe Spilewski, Bobb Biehl, Bill Lawrence, Aubrey Malphurs, Robert Waterman, and Steve Macchia.

And finally, to all those who have so powerfully led and served Camp of the Woods in Speculator, New York for so many years. It will forever be my home and my model of Hope!

ACKNOWLEDGMENTS

I once thought books were written by one person. Now? Not a chance! I realize anything that can be considered wise or a good idea likely came from someone else. Genius is knowing whom to steal from. I stole that line from Jim Dethmer! Since he said it, he likely stole it from someone as well!

However, there really are some people who have influenced this book, or actively helped me, and it would be unfair, wrong even, not to mention them. *And* by listing them, I can guarantee I'm leaving out other key people as well.

Note: Each person this book is dedicated to played an enormous role in influencing its content.

Gregg Stutts, Frank and Gayle Kelly, Patrick Snow, Tyler Tichelaar and Larry Alexander (editors), Brien Wloch (the real Brian in the story!), Haydee Chang, Beth Rech, Mia Davies, The BAM Center (Richard Roche, Denny Grim, Jim Mozdren, Robert Kostelny), Jim Candy, Larry Galley, Dan Galley, Ron Bryant, My Entrepreneur on Purpose MasterMind Groups, Glenn Schwartz, Ben and Brenda Peters, Doug and Doris Haugen, Jeff and Gail Fray, Eric and Liz Swanson, Dave Gibbons, Scott and Theresa Beck, Amy and Bill Pierson, Ed and Dusanka Armstrong, Ed and Margaret Williams, Dave and Carole Swaim, Ned and Beth Stevens, Jim and Carol Rumsey, Bob Purdy, Steve Nelson, Chuck and Anne Tomkins, Dave Burnham, Tom and Sharon Swing, Jane Leggett, Rick Harig, and Joe Grzelak.

Finally, to the town and people of Speculator, New York, the setting and inspiration for this book. May hope continue to flow for generations through this "all season vacationland."

"Once you choose hope, anything's possible."

— Christopher Reeve

CONTENTS

PREFACE

"The mountains are calling and I must go."

— John Muir, 1873

Every once in a while, we sense there's a voice calling us out of the valley and into the mountains. Call it grace, fate, or the voice of God—we get a glimpse of some bigger purpose, a destiny for our lives and a larger story being told. When we hear that voice, we shouldn't just stay where we are, but actually head out into the journey that seems weird, odd, or even a bit uncomfortable.

When we live in the valley or even the suburbs or plains, mountains speak of adventure, of beauty, of power, of meaning. They speak of hope for something transcending the mundane, the boring, and the blahs that create ruts we fall into and from which we can see no way out. They speak to our soul, whispering, "You have a bigger purpose."

For generations, the mountains have called us to come away in order to find what we might be missing in our day-to-day lives. As adventurers, we go to wild places where we need mountain guides to show us around. These mountain guides not only help us navigate the terrain, but they also help us see the incredible sights all around us and experience perspectives and vantage points we may otherwise have missed. These mountain experiences help us see ourselves and life again. They teach us to breathe—to experience beauty all around.

Still, most of us continue to get so caught up with living in the valleys that we settle for and accept the absence of hope or purpose. We become wired to get an education. Take tests. Get jobs. Make money. Don't go broke along the way.

We realize this isn't the way it's supposed to be, but we wonder, "What other way exists?" And maybe more practically...

"Who will guide me to something else?"

"Who will lead me away from the hurry and hopelessness into a better way?"

Very possibly, you've been sold false hope and fake beauty before. There's nothing worse than that—empty promises, lifeless religion, and phony gurus who make you ill.

But real hope? Sustainable hope with a vision for living out your unique purpose? That's something worth pursuing. And my guess is that's why you're reading this book. You want more. You're hungry to experience more in your life and breathe more of life in. And you are willing to take steps in that direction to learn, grow, and enter into new adventures. You're beyond the norm.

The good news? Mountains haven't left. The mountains still wait for you, and mountain guides can still help you see paths you've been missing and ways of life that won't just suck you dry, but instead empower you to experience fulfillment. Climbing those mountains will require learning self-leadership, but as you make real progress in that leadership journey, you will become a better version of you. Even more significantly, you will fulfill your God given purpose!

Just yesterday, I met with a ninety-one-year-old "mountain guide." When I was just ten years old, I got to know Mr. Spellmeyer. Later on, it was Dena Mortland. Then there was Harold Buirkle. I'll admit I still get teary-eyed thinking about them. And I've asked, "What if these mentors of hope were to reappear long enough not only to share what they see in us, but actually to share how we can learn to see what they see?"

What if those mountain guides showed up once again to help us deal with disappointments and process failures, or to help us get clarity and confidence back when we've been engulfed by fears? Most importantly, what if they showed us how to make hope the hallmark of our everyday life? Maybe even teach us how to take the next steps that will make all the difference so we can get back in the game, or change the game altogether?

If you've ever had the privilege of having great mentors, you know that they teach self-leadership as the starting point for all real leadership. They teach that greatness doesn't start or end on the outside, but on the inside. They encourage and inspire you to find out what works best and then learn not only to achieve dreams, but to do so while still loving our families, enjoying our lives, or even following God. Such mentors coach us not to remain stuck, discouraged, or even depressed, but to live within a vision of a hopeful future.

Have you met anyone like that? Encountered a mentor of hope? Someone who sees something in you and then does something that borders on the miraculous to call it out? Someone who tells you, "There's more out there! There's more in you than you know!"

This book was written for you to experience such an encounter with a mountain mentor in a place called Hope. If you've heard the call to come up to the mountains from your valley and you want to answer that call, my own hope is you'll not only be entertained, but you'll be inspired and empowered to get hope back and, ultimately, to fulfill the purpose and dreams you were created to fulfill.

If you've ever wondered whether a way of inspired and hopeful life exists that's not smoke, mirrors, and plastic, then you're in the right place. There will be some uphill travel and some fallen trees in the path, but the journey's worth it!

INTRODUCTION

"Take a breath. It's going to be okay."

— Bob Goff

None of us sets out to be discouraged or hopeless. And we certainly do not set out to become anything close to what could be called anxious or depressed! Midlife crisis? Relationship struggles? Job hatred? Who thinks it can happen to him or her? Yet, it happens to people even in their twenties! That's when I first started experiencing it. For others, it can be later in their fifties or sixties, or even later.

Life's way too short to spend years, even decades, being stuck or just consistently angry with ourselves or others. Yet 30 million Americans are currently on antidepressants and 250 million prescriptions for painkillers are written each year! The suicide rate just hit a thirty-year high. Billions in medical insurance dollars get spent each year treating the harvest of hopelessness. Gallup's State of the Global Marketplace study from 142 countries discovered that 63 percent of workers report being disengaged from their work, and a walloping 24 percent say they're "actively disengaged."

And when they come home, it's not much better! According to the National Opinion Research Center, 60 percent of people say they're "very unhappy" in their marriage. For the elderly, one out of five live in poverty. Even retirees with some money report being unhappy.

But the fact that you're reading a book titled *The Habits of Hope* says something powerful about you: You want something different! Better! You want to live your life, not let your life live you! And you don't want to be another statistic, nor live in fulfillment of what Benjamin Franklin said, "Some people die at twenty-five and aren't buried until they're seventy-five."

But that you are reading this book may also mean you've experienced something that I knew too well. Are you repeatedly discouraged about the way things are? Frustrated? Lacking consistent dreams and hopes of seeing things change for the better? Are you sick and tired of being sick and tired? Are you ready to make the pain go away and keep it from knocking at your door again?

I understand. I get it. I've been there, and I've written that book! I've had doctors diagnose me as anxious and depressed and prescribe medication as the only hope of keeping me from doing something drastic. I've dreaded Mondays because I couldn't bear to keep doing the work that felt so draining and pointless.

I've also been engaged with some notable people in positions of great power and prestige. I've skied at the best resorts in the world and vacationed at the Boca Beach Club. And I still felt empty.

On the other side, I've felt totally helpless as I proactively pushed my wife away, as my rage, disappointment, and self-hatred countered her best attempts to engage me with nothing but my selfish demands. Once extroverted and "people-person" me began dreading having to be with other people, even my very own family.

And then there's not being able to sleep through a night for years. Years! All the while, I stared at my Ivy League diploma along with my Masters of Theology degree hanging on the wall, as I sat in my black engraved alma mater chair. At one point, my card said I was the senior pastor of a growing church, but teaching others about peace, hope, and love was not enough to keep me from becoming chronically hopeless and deeply discouraged. I could never have imagined suicide as an alternative, but I did try to come up with ways to get relief from my reality.

When your life's not working, faith even feels hard to attain. You certainly don't want pious platitudes like, "Just have faith" or "It'll all work out."

No! You want real relief and change. A way out of the mess. And if someone does volunteer to come along and walk with you toward something better, you want to know that person has something authentic to offer and will definitely not judge you.

That's what I hope you experience as you read this book. I hope you see this as an encounter with a friend and coach who believes in you so much that he won't let you settle for something that's not you. And I would encourage you to take the book with you to a space in which you can breathe. Find a place where you can experience solitude, and open your mind and your spirit to learning these practical and tangible ways of discovering your own path to fulfilling your God-given purpose. Go to your own version of a mountain retreat and experience the mountain air. Let go of your to-do list, schedule, and smartphone for a bit, and breathe deeply as you explore. Journey into your own new and brighter future.

If you apply what you're about to learn and harness Habits of Hope, then my guess is you will become one of the people who gets to realize the power of hope and you will see this moment as a turning point to fulfill, or further fulfill, your God-given purpose. Depression and lasting discouragement can become something from your past, or even better, something you've heard of, but never had to walk through personally. You'll understand how to become someone who loves your work, finds fulfillment in your relationships, experiences life to the fullest, and becomes your spiritually alive self every single day.

As you'll see, this book is an inspirational fiction or allegory, and the main character's name is Gus. You'll experience his struggle to move from being chronically and routinely discouraged about life to something different. And, like many of us, Gus doesn't realize life can be different. Very different! Meaningful. Directed. Even powerful. At least he doesn't realize it *yet*. That's where Gus' encounter with Hope changes everything. It all starts with the self-leadership of his own life.

Of course you're apprehensive! You've likely tried things before. You've gone to motivational seminars. You've heard many talks and maybe even read books or heard sermons about hope, or fulfillment, or purpose. What's gonna make this any different? I would regularly proclaim to myself and my wife, Mindy, "I can't change! I've tried!" I even threw a gigantic theological book across my study, breaking the book and the wall! Yeah, it was memorable, but it didn't make me hopeful. Actually, I felt just the opposite!

My hope is that you will just allow the message of this book to mentor and coach you as you seek to apply the lessons from this story directly to your own life and situation. Open your mind to a new way of doing things that can breathe life into you now and continue to do so five years from now.

Are you ready to get started? Let's lock arms together and take this journey to Hope together. I'm so glad we're headed in that direction!

Jeff Colignon

CHAPTER 1

CONFUSED

"When you cease to dream, you cease to live."

— Malcolm Forbes

T he road ahead seemed to disappear as Gus did his best to keep driving through the fog.

Only Gus knew he had, just a couple of days earlier, seriously considered a quick tug of the wheel that would have caused him to swerve in front of the eighteen-wheeler in the oncoming lane.

"How did someone as normal as me become so messed up?" he wondered. He couldn't bring himself to such a final and stupid solution to his problems; however, he wanted the gnawing angst that was his life to change, and he no longer believed it could. Gus didn't have compelling answers or know where to turn.

Gus had long ago settled into the belief that things couldn't and wouldn't change, at least for him. This was his life. This was his career—if you could call it that. This was his marriage, tentative as it was. His mess. And he was stuck with all of it.

Though Gus no longer thought much about it, anyone who watched for a while might see that below the external din of Gus' life lurked the constant presence of a pervasive, gnawing, and never-changing anxiety.

Strip away the layers of angst and what you are left with is fear. Gus was afraid his life was going nowhere and his best years were behind him. He was afraid to change and afraid to stay the same. He was afraid of what others thought and afraid that he just didn't care what they thought.

Most of all, Gus was afraid that his life wasn't much more than a meaningless mess…and although he had started with such promise and hope, he had squandered all he'd been given and now was awash in a sea of blah—day in and day out survival.

If you were to ask Gus what role fear played in his life, he would have said, "Not much. Sure, I have some anxiety and get stressed at times, but fear? Not much more than the next guy."

Yet many of the decisions Gus made were run through a subtle grid that asked, "Is this safe?" "Will this keep me from pain?" "Will this protect my reputation?" "Will I be okay?"

The very atmosphere Gus grew up in, lived in, and accepted as the norm was infected with so much fear that Gus was just a shadow of whom he was meant to be. Gus just couldn't see it, nor detect its pervasive presence.

Now, as he drove home, the windshield wipers beat a dreary rhythm and smeared drizzle across the glass as he followed a blur of red taillights. The rain was just enough to keep the wipers going, but not enough to smooth the wiper blades' grating against the glass.

Some of the loneliest places in life exist within the echoing walls of one's own mind. Gus dreaded being alone, and he did what he could to interrupt his own thoughts by listening to the radio or rehearing responses to e-mail or texts in his head. Anything to keep from thinking deep thoughts.

The blurry lights and smeared window nauseated Gus and seemed to exacerbate his borderline headache and the aching fatigue he always felt at this time of the day. The radio just added more noise and bad economic news to the already angst-ridden moment. He'd been too busy to change those wiper blades, so every time it rained, Gus suffered through the distorted fog and pitied himself for failing to do something about it.

As Gus turned on the weather forecast, the reporter called for possible chances of showers during the evening. "Just my luck," he grumbled. "Route 59 is already slow because of construction. Rain isn't going to help."

Gus played the merging lanes game as he approached the intersection. As a fast-moving black SUV shoved in front of him, Gus bellowed, "Crap! Now, you'll get home two seconds before I do! *So* glad I could make your day, sir!" Of course, the driver couldn't hear him, but saying it out loud somehow allowed Gus to get back at the SUV driver…even if just in Gus' own mind.

Gus' mood was exacerbated by his chronic fatigue. Even copious amounts of caffeine during the day didn't seem to overcome the fatigue his inability to sleep caused. For as long as he could remember, he hadn't slept through a whole night. Night in and night out, he'd wake up around 3:00 a.m. and begin his regular worry-filled processing.

Sleep is an act of laying down what we can't control and trusting there's hope for tomorrow. But the hope-starved toss and turn— Gus was in that category.

Gus knew he should get in a workout, but getting back in the car to head to the gym felt like just one more "to do" in a day chockfull of to dos. "Oh, I guess I could just go for a short jog, but who wants to be out in the rain running? I don't need it that much! I'll go tomorrow," he thought to himself. Besides, he had skipped lunch today, so he didn't have many calories to work off. A half-dozen chocolate kisses on the run couldn't hurt much! Maybe just his cholesterol! He was ready for a good carb-packed dinner of Little Caesar's pizza and Crazy Bread.

While stuck in slow gear, Gus' mind rehearsed the day's events. More of the same junk. Though he knew it really didn't solve anything, he deliberated on what he "should" have said to Bruce Wilton when he complained that Gus must not see him as, "an important enough client to go out of your way." What Gus had wanted to say was: "You're right, Mr. Wilton.... I see it as my mission to make your life and my life miserable! It's such a pleasure to know I've succeeded! Would you want to refer any of your friends?"

Okay, so Gus would never really say that stuff—but tempted? Yes!

For the fearful, it tends to be oh, so much easier to see others as the problem than it is to face our own inner music. Fear has a way of helping us see the problem in "them" and their audacious selfishness with laser clarity. We see the problems, and they just grow in stature and significance the longer we stare at them, directly or indirectly.

Lately, Gus was spending more and more energy coming up with "getting even" scenarios. Of course, it wasn't helpful, but he felt some sick pleasure in it, and creating inner debates with no consequences whatsoever had become a habit for him. One of these days, he was afraid his cynicism would leak into some actual business meeting, but in the meantime, he kept his debates in his daydreams.

Gus had learned the hard way that even sharing them with his wife Amy did nothing but make her angry with him and leave him feeling more alone and disappointed with himself. Of course, complaining wasn't helpful. But he couldn't stop himself from rehearsing his disappointment both to himself, and at least once in a while, to Amy.

Gus tried to tell himself that things could always be worse. Compared to most of the planet, he was rich and had enough stuff and creature comforts to place him squarely in the "have" category. Others who had much more, however, would look at him as poor and pity him. The time he spent looking at things through their eyes only made his pity-party worse.

Things with Amy were gnawing at Gus, too, and he couldn't turn his mind off from her intolerance and bitterness toward him. A few nights before, she had said some words that had really pushed his buttons.

And his buttons had become more and more sensitive over time. Try as he might to make her happy, it just was never enough.

Just a couple of nights ago, following yet another snippy argument, Amy had looked him in the eye and said, "Sometimes, I wonder whether you understand the effect you have on me and the kids." With red and teary eyes, she had added, "I don't know how much longer I can live with your moods, your 'I hate my job; poor me' stuff. I can't remember the last time you were happy. Really happy! And to tell you the truth, I can't do anything about it. I've tried. It doesn't help. One of these days, you might just come home and find we've packed up and left. That might be better for all of us anyway."

"So what do you want me to do?" Gus had countered. "Do you think I'm in love with all that's going on? Do you think I don't wish things were different?"

Now the tears were trickling freely down Amy's face. "Gus, I sometimes wonder if the guy I married already died! Somewhere along the way, I think he may have. As sad as it is to say, I think you know it's true."

"Great!" he had said without even letting what she said sink in. "That's just great! And what am I supposed to do with that?"

"I really wish I could help you, Gus. I think you need to figure that out." Her tears had mixed with her mascara and dripped down, staining the carpet.

"So WHAT am I supposed to do!" Gus had yelled.

At that, she had done what Gus dreaded most. She had left. She had gotten in her car and left. He had no clue where she went. To a coffee shop? To a friend's house? He didn't know.

All he knew was, he was now alone—alone with Gus.

"Like you've got your act together!" Gus had shouted as she turned the corner. Of course, that really hadn't helped things; it had actually made him feel more alone. Desperate, Gus had kicked the grass and cussed.

With Amy gone, he felt really alone. Now what?

CHAPTER 2

THE LETTER

"Rock bottom became the solid foundation
on which I rebuilt my life."

— J.K. Rowling

Gus tried to block out the fight with Amy as he drove. He knew she was still angry with him, but apologies no longer worked the way they once did. Things with the kids weren't that bad, but they weren't on a great trajectory either. Nothing had quite prepared him for the lack of respect they showed him now that they were in their teens. The worst part was when they rolled their eyes at him. That had begun with his oldest, and now it even infected the youngest. "Sure, Dad! You go do that!" Getting angry at them only seemed to stoke their disrespect for him. They didn't spend much time with him anymore. Their friends! It was all about their friends! Whatever happened to just being with the family?

Finally, after hitting every red light in the state, Gus turned down his street and headed toward the house. He lived in one of those late '80s subdivisions with the basketball net in every driveway, the well cared for lawns, and neighbors who pretty much kept to themselves.

As usual, he drove past the driveway and pulled over to the mailbox. He lowered his window and reached out to haul in the typical bundle of junk mail, magazines, and bills. As he flipped through them, separating the supermarket throwaways from the keepers, something unusual caught his attention. Unlike the typical computer-generated type in the stack, this one was handwritten. "What in the world?" he said out loud. He stared in wonder at the somewhat yellowed business envelope through squinted eyes.

This thing looked like it had been through too many post offices. It contained a small pile of yellow forwarding address stickers and green "No such address" stamps, and yet clear as day, he saw his name written in all capital letters.

GUS JOHNSON

Gus also observed that the stamp on the envelope appeared to be a relic as well. He noticed the twenty-nine cent stamp and wondered out loud who might have put that antique on there? "I can't remember when stamps went for that!"

What shocked him most was the return address. Stunned, he read: R. Turnquest.

"R. Turnquest!" he exclaimed! "Rodney Turnquest?" But, as best he could remember, Mr. Turnquest had died sometime in the 1990s!

It couldn't be from him! How could he be getting a letter from Mr. Turnquest?

Gus put the car in park and studied the envelope. This thing must have spent the last decade trapped in some dusty post office somewhere. Underneath his current address, he noticed an address he hadn't lived at in years. Under that, another previous address. *I don't think I could remember that address if my life counted on it*, he thought. Then, he ripped open the top and pulled out a handwritten letter on yellowed stationery.

Sure enough, it said Mr. and Mrs. Rodney W. Turnquest on the top and listed their Hope, New York, address. Memories flooded Gus' mind. The Turnquests. Hope, New York. "I haven't heard from them in years! And they are dead, aren't they?"

Gus recognized Mr. Turnquest's handwriting:

> Dear Partner,
>
> (*He was the only one who called Gus that…from the time he was a kid!*)
>
> I am in a hurry to get this to you. Please forgive the inconvenience. I left something for you in my safety deposit box in Hope, NY. I told Mrs. Wright you would come for it. I am enclosing the key.
>
> Warmly,
>
> Your Friend,
>
> R. Turnquest

Gus' mind raced. Just hearing from Mr. Turnquest was strange enough. But he couldn't recall for sure when Turnquest had died; he vaguely remembered it being in the early or mid-1990s. It seemed like a long time ago. Sadly, in all his busyness, Gus hadn't found the time to attend the funeral or even send condolences to Mr. Turnquest's wife. As far as Gus knew, she had also passed away.

So what could Mr. Turnquest possibly have left for me in a safety deposit box in Hope? And why didn't he just put it in the envelope? Gus thought.

Gus certainly knew Hope well. It was a tiny town up in the Adirondacks with one small grocery store, a corner ice cream parlor, and a general store that sold everything from propane to ponchos and popcorn. Gus had spent several summers there in his youth, and even worked at Camp of the Woods at the foot of Hope Mountain as a teenager.

Gus hadn't heard or thought much about Hope, New York, in many years, but it did bring back memories of summers spent up there in his youth.

That's really one of the most beautiful places on earth, he thought. He thought of the clarity of Lake Hope, the awesome aroma of fresh pine in the air, the brilliant starry-skied nights, the green mountains, and all the fun in what was called (at least by the sign) "All Season Vacationland."

So what did Mr. Turnquest leave in a safety deposit box? For a moment, Gus fantasized that it was some kind of inheritance. He remembered thinking the Turnquests had a lot of money, but he also knew that they lived very simply. Maybe he had put something valuable in there that he wanted Gus to have. *A large check could come in quite handy*, Gus thought.

Gus re-read the note, looking to see whether he could find any clues as to what Turnquest had left him. The only other thing in the envelope was a small, gold key Scotch-taped to the letter. It wasn't as if Hope, New York, were the next town away or anything. Now that he lived in the Midwest, getting back to that area involved either a flight or a whole day of driving. He didn't think he'd ever just be driving through Hope any time soon.

CHAPTER 3

HESITATING

"Everything you've ever wanted is on the other side of fear."

— George Adair

As the rain started picking up its pace, Gus closed the car window and stuffed the letter and key back in the envelope. He took a long, deep breath. Time for some Little Caesars pizza. He carefully pulled the car into the garage, then headed inside the house where Julius, his white German Shepherd, barked and greeted him with his typical enthusiasm. "At least someone is still glad to see me when I get home," he said, patting Julius on the head.

Then, along with the pile of papers and bills, he crunched the letter in the kitchen "stuff drawer." It was time to forget the day and relax. Amy was nowhere to be seen.

September in the Midwest offers a tossup between magnificent sunny days and cloudy days that remind everyone that winter looms just over the horizon. A few yellowing trees provide subtle hints that things are in flux, even though the grass remains green and the days are still long enough. September is packed with back to school nights, school sports, and carpools for the kids, and in business, everything that had been put on hold until after Labor Day. Though most adults aren't back in school, they act as if the fall semester has now begun. It's as if someone has hit fast forward on the time button and the days and weeks accelerate rapidly. Get your assignments done or face bad grades!

Gus continued to live in the fog of low grade fatigue, but he didn't have much chance to do anything about it. His workouts continued to be sacrificed most nights, and after dinner, he was pretty much ready to "veg" on the couch, watch CNN and some ESPN, maybe a movie, then get to bed. Each morning, the alarm clock hit him with a painful reminder of responsibility and the day began again.

Things with Amy didn't improve, and though she finally came back home after a few days gone to who knows where, things were icy at best. Though Gus and she didn't have any blow ups, they didn't talk much either—maybe just to report in on whose job it was to take the kids here or there. Almost just like being bad roommates.

Gus periodically remembered Mr. Turnquest's letter, usually when he put something else into the stuff drawer. At first, like a lot of things, he just felt, "I can't deal with this now." But when business margins seemed tight, he started to wonder, "Am I crazy for not even checking this out?" He started to think more and more about the letter, particularly when stuck in traffic. "I really could use a windfall about now," Gus said to the snarled traffic.

Gus never did share the letter with Amy—partly because he felt weird about the whole thing, and partly because he didn't know how she would react. He was afraid she would force him to get in the car and head straight to Hope, New York. But Amy tended to stay clear of that junk drawer, so Gus knew she wouldn't find the letter.

One day, over coffee at Starbucks with his buddy Brian, Gus finally brought up the whole strange situation.

Brian's response actually surprised him.

"You're crazy, Gus! If I were you, I'd be in that car right now heading for Hope! Who knows what's in that box! Isn't curiosity killing you?"

"But, Brian," Gus protested, "what if it's nothing? I can't afford a two-day trip to get one of Mr. Turnquest's poems or some article. He used to cut stuff out and give it to me—as if some sort of motivational snippet was going to change my life! What if it's just another one of those?"

"I hear you," Brian agreed. "But as usual, I'm going to give you my unsolicited advice. I think you should check it out. What's the worst that can happen?"

"What's the worst that can happen?" Gus repeated.

CHAPTER 4

HEADING TO HOPE

"Not all those who wander are lost."

— J.R.R. Tolkien in *Lord of the Rings*

September rolled into October and Gus thought more about the letter and the key. Part of him was afraid of the disappointment if what he found in the box wasn't worth the trip. However, he also knew there was something out there for him, and if he never got it, he'd always wonder.

And the truth was, the chances of him just happening to drive unintentionally through Hope were slim to none. If he were going to see what he'd been left, he had to make a purposeful journey to Hope.

His opportunity came the week before Columbus Day. Gus had a conference in Cleveland, where he'd give a presentation on

Thursday, and he planned to stay through for the remainder of the conference. But he could skip out after his talk! Cleveland was closer to upstate New York than to his home—maybe eight hours or so? He wouldn't even have to tell anyone where he was going. He'd just plan on getting back home a little later Friday night.

For some reason, he felt sneaky about the whole thing, so he didn't even tell Brian. He stuck the letter with the key in his briefcase and headed to Cleveland. When he finished his talk, he loaded up things in the car and checked out of his room.

"Okay, Mr. Turnquest, you've got my attention!"

The drive on Route 90 west toward New York was actually magnificent that day: high sixties, blue sky, and the color of the autumn trees, particularly as he entered New York, were dramatic and soothing. Gus rolled the windows down and turned up the music, tuning into an oldies station.

It dawned on him that some of the songs were the very ones he had listened to when growing up and spending summers in the Adirondacks. Pleasant memories of simpler and kinder times. He breathed a sigh of longing.

As he headed toward the Pennsylvania line, Gus recalled what he could about Rodney Turnquest:

Rodney Turnquest had lived near Gus' family in New Jersey, but he also had a summer home up in the Adirondacks, just across Lake Hope from Gus' family's summer home. Gus' parents had known Mr. Turnquest from when they were young.

Mr. Turnquest was "a character." Or maybe the whole phrase, "He's a real character." Gus didn't think he had ever been in Mr. Turnquest's presence when Mr. Turnquest didn't have some joke or story to share. Gus liked the stories about Mr. Turnquest's infamous pranks best.

Mr. Turnquest's house was always filled with guests and parties—cookouts, somewhat illegal fireworks on the Fourth of July, too many people crammed onto his two pontoon party boat, and a laugh that clearly announced he was in the room.

Teenagers were always at the Turnquests' house during the summer. Even after the Turnquests' own kids were grown and married, their home was still the gathering place for teens. And they had all the best stuff to play with. A giant trampoline on their lawn, a tether ball, a paddle boat, and even one of the original sand volleyball pits.

Gus also remembered how Mr. Turnquest used to show up at his own high school football games. Whether it was freshman, JV, or varsity, he was one of the non-family members who would regularly come to Gus' games. How had he forgotten about that?

Mr. Turnquest was that rare adult who didn't appear too busy to care.

In a world where most people go about their own business and keep to themselves, what would make an adult invest in a little kid?

Gus remembered a quote from Forest E. Witcraft that hung on a friend's wall: "A hundred years from now it will not matter what my bank account was, the sort of house I lived in, or the kind of car

I drove…but the world may be different because I was important in the life of a child."

Gus couldn't recall what Mr. Turnquest had done for a living, but from what he had heard, he had given away much of his money and chosen to live very simply. He would typically boat over to the other side of the lake where his small, but tastefully decorated, home sat, hidden in the trees on a hill.

As Gus thought about it, he could see a number of eight by ten wood-framed, colored photographs. These were pictures of Mr. and Mrs. Turnquest on trips to Alaska, Hawaii, and the Middle East. Pictures of family and friends around a campfire. Pictures of Mr. and Mrs. Turnquest in Africa surrounded by a host of smiling tribal people celebrating the creation of a clean water well.

Then, of course, there were Mr. Turnquest's famous notes. From as far back as Gus could remember, Mr. Turnquest regularly gave him an encouraging note or quote. He would have them in a sealed envelope and say, "Partner, this is something for you."

"Thanks, Mr. Turnquest," Gus would say very politely. Then Gus would stuff the note in his pocket. He'd long since lost the last of them, or he had left them at his parents' home as a relic of days gone by. Words. That was all they were. Words on a page. Yet now as an adult himself, Gus thought to himself that he could never imagine writing to a kid. But why not? What was missing in him that made him so different from Rodney Turnquest?

CHAPTER 5

WELCOME TO HOPE

"If you lose hope, somehow you lose the vitality that keeps life moving, you lose that courage to be, that quality that helps you go on in spite of it all. And so today I still have a dream."

— Martin Luther King, Jr.

T he trees along the lakes and rivers near the road were ablaze with color. Mixing that with the smell of pine coming through the open windows caused Gus to find himself breathing deeply.

As he took deep breaths, he started to realize that somewhere in the last few years, he'd quit breathing. Amid all of life's stress, schedules, junk with Amy, and everything else, he couldn't recall the last time he had just breathed deeply for the simple pleasure of filling his lungs with life.

What makes someone stop breathing deeply as a regular practice? What makes him miss the simple pleasures of fresh air and a sunny day?

The road toward Hope winds and twists around all kinds of gullies, crosses rivers, and cuts around mountains. After heading through the small town of Piseco, with its sign for the regional airport, and past Oxbow Lake, Gus drove into Hope, with its classic "Welcome to Hope—All Season Vacationland" sign. No one would ever consider replacing the '50s-looking snowmobile, the bear, and the deer. Some things never change! Classic.

Rounding from Route 8 onto Route 30, Gus passed the "famous" Hope Department Store, Chas. Johns Store, Adirondack Market, King of the Frosties, the town baseball field, and Camp of the Woods. All these places packed memories of simpler times and fun in this "all season vacationland."

Gus felt grateful that these places still existed. He started to think, "What might it be like to just pack up and move here for who knows how long?" This sure seemed like a simpler life. A better life.

Again, more memories of his youth filled his head. The famous Fourth of July parade…. The flea market during the day and carnival at night, with booths selling snow cones, cotton candy, caramel apples, and rides, including a gigantic Ferris wheel. He pictured his first real crush and their "date" to watch the fireworks on the town beach. How he had held her hand as the fireworks echoed off the mountains, replaying each giant boom.

Gus pulled into the parking lot at Hope National Bank, looked around, and reminded himself why he had traveled all this distance.

With one small step, he got out of the car, taking the key and the original letter with him, almost as security to prove who he was and why he was there. Part of him felt like he'd stolen something that wasn't his. Had he?

The Letter

Gus just walked in as if he knew where he was going, and he quickly eyed the safety deposit box area. There were a couple of customers in the bank, so he hoped he could sneak in and out undetected.

Gus found the number on the key and matched it with box seventy-seven. Sure enough, the box opened and there it was: An envelope with his name on it. He took a deep breath and opened it.

The letter was written on white stationery without lines. Though it was handwritten, it was so neat and straight across the page that it may as well have been typed. He held the pages in his hand and felt his heart beating as he took a deep breath and began to read.

> Dear Partner,
>
> I realize you weren't expecting to hear from me. You're probably wondering why in the world I would be writing to you. I don't blame you. But you're curious, aren't you? At least curious enough to venture to Hope and open a bank vault. That really does say a lot about you. Curiosity is a good quality. Without it, the world would be a much duller place.
>
> The fact you're reading this means you really are a seeker. I respect that quality in you! Has anyone else ever referred

to you like that before? A seeker? I once saw a bumper sticker that said, "Not all who wander are lost." I like that! Seekers are the ones who make the rest of us a whole lot more human. They refuse to turn off that wondering voice inside their heads.

Even if it's the voice that asks "why?" only to be met by silence. You refuse to settle for life at face value…. You can't put life in a box of success defined by someone else. You're the one who pushes the envelope of what's accepted and acceptable. You see the world as impressive and incredible but also disappointing and dismal. You see hypocrites and get bugged. You see the rich and famous and ask, "Why are they so messed up?" You see the religious and ask, "Who wants to be like them?" You experience pain and loss in life and ask, "Is there a better way?"

Not all those who wander are lost.

And you doubt. You doubt the simple and simplistic answers you were taught. You doubt that life is meaningful. You doubt that God has a bigger purpose for your life. Maybe you doubt that God even exists. You doubt that good gets rewarded. Maybe good guys really do just finish last.

Okay, so you're still wondering: Why is Mr. Turnquest writing to me? Are these the philosophical musings of a crazy old man? Well, maybe. I've been called worse! You may have already heard that my time on this earth is coming to an end. The doctors seem to think I only have a short time left….

So the bottom line is this—I am writing to you because of your destiny. That's right. This letter is meant to unlock the secret to the life of Hope you were born for.... Your destiny, Gus. <u>You've been called.</u>

I had a dream and I saw your face in the future. Your face was beaming. You looked so, so pleased. Fulfilled. You were fully alive. Vibrant!

It was what I saw in you when you were just a boy. It's what made me realize there was something special about you.

In the dream, you recognized that your life had purpose—a bigger purpose. The very purpose you were born for was to be fulfilled. And Gus, you were affecting a revolution of God-sized change in the world.

I know, you're wondering, what's this old guy thinking? Me? How can that be?

I didn't know if I'd ever see you again, so I needed to get this down on paper. And you know how much I love giving you notes, right? Somehow, I came to believe you really needed to hear this message. God needed you to hear this message. It was important, really, really important.

You know how dreams can have different scenes? Different sections. The first scene was of you thriving. Alive. Courageous. Free to be you. But then it was almost as if I stepped into you in a totally different scene.

It was a dark, almost unnatural place. There you were again.

But this time you looked beaten down. Burdened. Your body looked weak and you were thirsty. Then I saw where you were: you were in a dry, dusty, and bleak desert. As I watched you, you walked away from me—walking alone in this terrible desert.

Then you came across a valley. There was something in the valley and you moved down into it to see what it was. The valley was filled with dry bones. At first, you were taken back by the sight. But your curiosity kicked in. As you examined them, you discovered some of the bones had slight signs of flesh, but most were simply lifeless. They were dry, cracked, brittle, or in the process of turning to dust. Some were hardly visible beneath the dust. You looked confused and discouraged.

What were these dry bones? What were they doing in the valley? You looked up into the sky and said out loud, "What are these dry bones?"

Surprisingly, a voice from heaven answered you.

"These bones are the destinies of my people. They're the destinies of the living."

"But they're dead, disgusting bones!" you actually shouted at God. "They're totally dead, buried, and turning to dust!"

I could see the look on your face. You looked puzzled. Confused. "I don't have a destiny!" you said. "Destinies are the naïve beliefs of foolish people not living the tough stuff of everyday life! There must be something wrong!"

"No," the voice answered. "These destinies can live again. Do you believe they can live?"

Then I saw something else in your face. Not just confusion. First it was a dark, doubting disappointment, as if you should have never been put in a place like this. What were you doing in this valley filled with decaying and dry bones? Then it was as if the look on your face turned to frustration and you became angry…but you couldn't bring yourself to share that emotion. Finally, you said, "I have no idea. I have no idea if there's any use for bones!"

Then the voice spoke again. "Do you want these bones to live? If you do, ask them to come back to life. Speak to them, and ask them to breathe again. Don't you want them to come back to life?"

You just stood there for what seemed like an eternity. You were shaking.

That's when I woke up. It was nothing like anything I'd ever experienced. Most nights when I dream, it's quite forgettable. Not this dream! This was something quite unusual.

Partner, I know this seems pretty strange to you. It felt strange to me too. I felt like I had no choice but to share this message with you. It was as if I suddenly realized that it must be some kind of message for you. You must be living in a confusing world, and you must need a message of hope. You have some sort of destiny to fulfill…something to add to the bigger picture of what's happening in the world.

But I sense there's something holding you back. There's something that stands in the way of you living into your bigger purpose…and helping others live into theirs. You just have no idea how to get from where you are to where you're destined to go…to whom you're destined to be. What you're destined to accomplish.

Let me pause here: I think I know you well enough to have an idea of what you're probably thinking.

First, "This is really bizarre!"

Secondly, "Why me?"

To the first thought, I can only say, "Aren't a lot of things in life bizarre?" Like why are we even alive in the first place? Why were we born where we were born? Why have we been given all the opportunities we have so far?

But I believe there's something standing in the way… something you've got to chase down that stands like a giant wall between where you are now and the purpose you were born for.

Let the fact that you're reading these words get through to the deepest part of you right now.

Your time has come. It's time to let the true you emerge. It's your time to engage your bigger purpose. You have more to offer a desperate world than you think. If you aren't free to be fully you, you lose. Those who love you lose. The world loses.

Pay attention! For too long you bought into the lie that you had nothing special to offer the world. You didn't think you were created for any important work...maybe you wondered whether you were even created at all. I get that. Partner, you can either get busy living or get busy dying. Which do you want?

I am forever your loyal friend.

Fondly, Rodney Turnquest

When Gus took his eyes off the letter, his hands were clammy and shaking. His first thought was, "You're right Mr. T. Why me?"

CHAPTER 6

DECIDING TO STAY

"It is not the mountain we conquer, but ourselves."

— Sir Edmund Hillary

It was hard to believe that Mr. Turnquest expended the time to do this...that he dreamed about Gus wailing in a valley of dry bones. That he wrote such a letter so close to his own death. That he had taken the time to stick it in a safety deposit box in Hope, New York, and had Gus drive all the way to upstate New York to get it!

"But what do I do with this?" Gus said, referring to the letter he still held.

At the same time, Gus also felt an odd sense of being extremely cared for. In another way, he felt exposed. Like someone who knew the real him had broken into his brain and addressed the questions bouncing around in his lonely head. As he read the letter, he felt known—reached out to.

Some of the phrases were the exact ones he had mulled over. But he had gotten used to dismissing them as the naïve or frustrating stuff he had to let go. He blocked them as unhelpful in an insipid and uninteresting life.

"You must be living in a confusing world, and you must need a message of hope. You have some sort of destiny to fulfill…something to add to the bigger picture of what's happening in the world."

That was the tug—feeling like he was here for a purpose, but being clueless and confused as to what the purpose could or should be!

There was something inside of Gus that wanted to consider the big things in life. But where in our busy lives do we get to think about such big questions? Purpose. Destiny. And then there's the problem…. What if you think the deep thoughts and don't find any real answers?

Mr. Turnquest was right. Gus had given up believing, and he knew it. And with the mess that was his life, he had given up searching.

Was this an invitation to find what he'd been looking for, even though he hadn't known where to search before?

Gus found himself in a quandary. It was the beginning of Columbus Day weekend, and he was in what he sometimes referred to as "Nowhere, New York." The sun was setting, and to drive home, or even part of the way home, felt like a heavy burden. He remembered a song from an old English punk rock band, the Clash, "Should I stay or should I go?"

For many years, doing something just for himself wasn't part of Gus' way of being. He had a family to care for and had largely stopped caring for himself. To stay felt somewhat self-indulgent, and he knew he'd need to spend some money for a room.

Though Gus had been depleted of energy, physically, emotionally, and certainly spiritually, he had never made the connection between times of intentional solitude and experiencing nature with getting more energy or rebuilding his own creativity and life-direction.

Some years ago, his friend Brian had given him a book called *Caring for Your Own Soul*. Gus had read parts of the book, but he felt such a way of life full of solitude and meditation seemed more suited to monks and missionaries than most men he knew, including himself. Besides, in a dog-eat dog world, who had time for such frivolous things? And these days, Gus was all about functional.

Yet the book's message came back to him as he wrestled with whether to do the functional and head back home, or stay in Hope for the night, or even the long weekend. "What does it benefit a man if he gains the whole world and forfeits his very soul?" Gus recalled these words from Jesus himself. Did they have any connection to his day-to-day life, or was it just a religious text that only had to do with what happens when you die?

Most of Gus' religious experiences had seemed to be about that—a morbid preoccupation with death. The creeds talked a lot about the hereafter, but not so much about what to do in the meantime. Somehow, spirituality felt so foreign to Gus' everyday concerns about making money, keeping a business going, and getting his marriage to work.

Gus felt a war going on inside himself. To choose to stay in the Adirondacks now that he had accomplished what he had come for, opening that safety deposit box, seemed to go against the grain of his bottom line existence. He had never attended any kind of retreat, except maybe Camp of the Woods where he went with his family when he was a boy. He was close to Camp of the Woods now, and good memories of extended spiritual input came back to him. Whole weeks had been spent with his family surrounded by people, including Mr. Turnquest, who seemed to take their own spiritual development seriously.

Certainly, Gus didn't see the idea of a retreat as a way to find his way home or to experience God in the realities of his own life. His spiritual practices lacked any vision to do what Elizabeth Kübler-Ross called learning to "get in touch with the silence within yourself and know that everything in this life has a purpose."

Aristotle had said, "Knowing yourself is the beginning of all wisdom." What if he was right?

Gus got in his car and headed up toward Melody Lodge, a quaint, rustic inn overlooking Lake Hope with a striking view of Hope Mountain. He had decided this was going to be his weekend away—this was going to be his time to get his soul back in order and find what he'd been missing for so long.

CHAPTER 7

THE CANOE TRIP

"Making a big life change is pretty scary.
But know what's even scarier? Regret."
— Zig Ziglar

After checking into his second floor room, Gus went to the dining room to enjoy the Melody Lodge's famous rack of lamb. Then Gus decided to head out and reinvestigate the town he had loved so much in his youth.

First stop—Camp of the Woods.

The full moon glistened off the mountains as Gus walked barefoot on the beach in front of Camp of the Woods. The beach was one of the longest white sand beaches Gus had ever seen. It glistened a soft gray in the moonlight, and the lake reflected the dark shades of the mountains. Gus could hear the sound of loons as well as his own breathing in the perfect stillness.

Gus recalled campfires scenes he had enjoyed on this beach as a teen working for the camp. Cool breeze days staffing at the Rec. Shack. Daily Chapel services at the Tibbits auditorium. Sticky buns and "Mr. Steve" drinks. Meeting friends at the Tee Pee after concerts. Then there were the walks with some of the girls he had dated here, sitting on the wall hand-in-hand, watching shooting stars. His future had seemed so bright and far away then.

It was hard not to wish those times had never ended. Sure, he was pretty cocky about his future then, and maybe he had even fooled the girls into thinking he knew what he wanted. Maybe he had known. Maybe not. He wasn't as sure now. All he knew was that those days seemed so much more hopeful.

Gus knew he'd had some kind of faith in those years. It was at least one of convenience. Chapel speakers preaching through the teachings of Bible. Songs sung from a hymnal...sitting arm-and-arm next to Janine...Cathy...Christa...wondering whether he could get away with flirting during the message.

But he did have some spiritual moments—some late night conversations, some "there's a big God out there" feelings. Yet the pre-curfew walks along the beach still held something for him. The ghosts of those moments still seemed present somehow as he walked, stopping to take off his shoes and let his feet feel the cool sensation of the sand. He came to a little flow of water coming through the sand from a pipe and sloshed right through it. It was ice cold, likely coming from runoff up in the hills.

Gus found himself longing for those summer romances. He wasn't sure it was even the girls he missed. Maybe it was the longing for a young, positive outlook. Hope. That's what he missed. He missed the optimistic guy who believed that life could be good. He missed being believed in by adults. He missed being someone special in someone's eyes…even his own eyes.

Gus basked in the feeling of the cool sand on his feet, which created a feeling of awareness that his typical, shoe-clad self had been missing for years. He kicked the sand as he walked, moving toward the lake and then dipping his toes in.

"Wow! Definitely cold!" With the warmness of the day, Gus had forgotten it was early October and no longer August. He moved back to the beach, but then he was unable to see the water ripples emanating from the spot where he had dipped his foot into the lake so he returned to the water's edge and again touched his toe to its surface and watched the water ripple away from him.

He walked on. As he walked, he happened upon a flipped canoe. It was an aluminum Grumman, and just his luck, the wood paddle jutted from beneath the overturned boat.

Once again, good memories of late night canoe trips…laughing on the still water, a stealth invasion of the island girl's camp to wreak some good-natured havoc. A little posse of friends had actually hauled a giant pair of men's underwear—well, really a jock-strap— up the camp's flagpole after midnight in one foray.

Gus smiled, wondering about that morning when the girls did their daily flag-raising ceremony. He had never heard what had happened. Maybe the camp had a "Don't publicize terrorists" mentality, and didn't want to give the pranksters the joy of hearing the whole story.

He could only imagine the shrieks from the girls that morning—Miss Jane turning bright red!

Then, almost instinctively, Gus seized the paddle, flipped the canoe, and hauled it off to the water. He jumped in and was off. This was going to be fun! Who would ever know? He could just paddle out to the island in the middle of the lake, maybe around it, and then come back. No one would miss him or the canoe for an hour or so.

The canoe cut a gentle ripple through the water, and the only sound he could hear was the whoosh and the dripping of the paddle. The beauty of the huge sky, the full moon, and the peaceful silence practically engulfed him as he moved through the water. He felt some guilt for taking the canoe, but that ceased quite easily since he would return it and no one would ever know it had been borrowed—no, enjoyed—for a late evening tour. Besides, who wouldn't understand how much he was in need of some kind of enjoyment?

Gus had been through a lot!

He had tried so hard to make his life count for something! When others had been out getting ahead in business, he was seeking to serve people. He was working with a non-profit. He was trying to help people in need and help them find "the truth!"

It wasn't his fault they didn't want it! It wasn't his fault that giving his all just wasn't enough. So he wasn't successful. And now he had to pay the price. For what? For trying? For believing that he could make a difference?

Sure, "most people exist; that is all." At this time in life, he just wanted to exist…if even that—sometimes, not even that.

The tug of war continued inside. He really did want to give his life to something that mattered. But to him, it felt like despite his good intentions, he was left alone and uncelebrated. Who cared that he had once cared? He certainly felt like God didn't care. And if God did, God certainly was pretty silent about it.

Gus realized how quickly his mind snapped back to "Poor me!" He had gone from enjoying the incredible surroundings to wallowing in his own despair. It was as if his two selves took turns talking inside his head. And often the "poor me" won the day and overcame the other guy. How he hated that about himself! But for whatever reason, he just felt stuck with that.

Breaking free from being stuck. That was what he longed for. But how? How?

Gus thought he was about halfway out to the island. For whatever reason, most tend to lose all sense of distance in the middle of a lake. He recalled numerous times losing his way in the early morning fog, while trying to navigate out to the island—feeling completely clueless as to where he was or which direction to go.

In many ways, this feeling of being lost in the fog felt like his current situation. He felt foggy, directionless. Without even trying, he was just kind of wandering around, clueless.

Gus was a bit tired, so he decided to take a breather and relax for a few minutes. He pulled his paddle in, and in doing so, he knocked the side of the canoe in the dark, fumbled the paddle into the water, and tried to grab it all in one movement.

Almost instantly, Gus felt gravity shift, and in a split second, he found himself plunging headfirst into the water, with the canoe flipping on top of him. In an instant, his calm canoe trip turned into a freezing cold nightmare in the darkness of the lake.

The frigid water snatched his breath, and Gus struggled to the surface, pushing the canoe away with the side of his head. Whack! "NO!" he shouted.

He could feel his head throb, but he was caught up in the rush of adrenaline as the sudden change in circumstances mixed with the shock of the cold water.

"Okay, calm yourself. Calm yourself! You've got to get back in that canoe. You've got to get back," Gus told himself. With all his might, he pushed at the canoe, trying to right it as he tread water. "What was I thinking? How could I get upright when I had no hard ground to stand on?" But he tried again. And again. "Darn it! Darn it!" he shouted.

His breaths felt dangerously short as he summoned his strength.

"HELP! HELP!" he called.

He waited and listened. Nothing. Again he called with all he could. "Help! In the lake!" Again, he came back to the, "Calm yourself thoughts."

"What would survivor-man do now?" he wondered. No episodes of flipped canoes came to mind.

"Should I leave the canoe and swim? Is it even possible to get to shore?"

Then a terrible thought hit him. "What if I don't make it? Will my body even be found? Who knows I'm here?" And then even more clearly: "I can't leave my family. I can't leave Amy! I love her. She needs me. My sons. They need me. They need me."

Gus had heard that you become quite clear about what matters most in moments like these. He had heard that in a film about a guy who had been trapped for 127 hours in a cave and had to cut his arm off: Aaron Ralston. He had read it in a book written by a guy trapped in a hotel in Haiti after an earthquake.

"I don't want to leave my family. No. Not just disappear. Not just have my kids grow up without a dad! I never even told Amy I was heading up here!"

Then, in the midst of the stress and the cold water, the worst possible thing happened. Gus' right leg cramped. A powerful contraction in Gus' calf shot instant pain through his body.

"Awwwww!" he shouted in pain—flailing wildly in the water.

"Don't let it end this way. Please, God! Don't let me just miss out on my own life. And even more, others need me! Don't let them have to live without me! Please, God! I want my life back! Please, God! Help me! Please!"

Gus knew he had to keep moving. He had to overcome the resistance—it would just cause him to give up and not move forward toward what mattered most. It was all about being able to live for those he cared most about. And at that moment, despite all the evidence he had given to the contrary, he realized he did want to live.

Again, he summoned all his strength.

"Help! Help!"

He felt his head throb and realized he was getting a little lightheaded.

"Oh, God, this isn't good," he said. "Just keep going. You can't give up," he urged himself on. "You can make it! This doesn't have to be the end! Live, Gus! Live! Live!"

CHAPTER 8

RESCUED

"Having someone wonder where you are when you don't come home at night is a very old human need."

— Margaret Mead

Gus was never one to wear any kind of flotation device, particularly since he had been an excellent swimmer for as long as he could remember. The lake may not have appeared cold enough to kill a grown man, at least not quickly, but what Gus was experiencing was common to those who drown in water they may have survived in for much longer. First, he had a hard time breathing. It was a "cold shock" that practically incapacitated him, rapidly increasing his heart rate and lowering his blood pressure.

Next, though Gus could tread water for long periods, without adequate insulation in his body, his core temperature dropped, bringing blood from the veins in the extremities and actually constricting those veins to protect his vital organs. As that happened, Gus began to lose his ability to control his hands, and the muscles in his arms and legs quit working well enough to keep him above water.

The lake was colder than usual for the time of year, even though it had warmed up some in the last few days. First, he had a hard time breathing. It was "cold shock" that practically incapacitated him, rapidly increasing his heart rate and lowering his blood pressure.

Gus shivered almost uncontrollably at first, his body trying to offset the loss of heat. But his mind and his muscles quickly started to deteriorate in the cold water and darkness.

Gus began to think, "Can this really be it?" Each of his kids came to his mind. Amy. Would anyone ever even find his body? Who would know he was out here?

T.S. Eliot had once said, "It is worth dying to find out what life is." Was dying what was now happening to Gus out in the middle of the lake?

"Grab my hand! Here! Can you see me? Can you see me at all? Grab my hand! Right here. Grab my hand!"

Gus had no idea where the voice was coming from; he wondered whether he was hallucinating. Or was it God? Gus recalled hearing that when some people have died and come back, they later recalled seeing a light beckoning to them. A tunnel. Maybe even Jesus or God. "Grab my hand," however, didn't seem like a message from God.

Gus gathered his strength and reached up, but in complete darkness and without any visual reference, he just groped. He tried telling his arms to move, but still he bobbed under the water as if paralyzed. Nothing worked.

Gus breathed with gasping riffs, frantic to get air back into his lungs and even coughing out the frigid water. Was he dreaming? Had someone really come along to save him? Or was this what death was like?

Strong arms reached down and enveloped Gus, first around the shoulders, then grabbing his arms…as if someone else were in the water with him.

"Don't fight me! Please, don't fight me! I'm here to help!"

Almost by some bizarre instinct, Gus couldn't help himself. He flailed so wildly, trying to save himself, that he threatened to drown himself and his rescuer.

Why was this such a gut instinct for Gus? Salvation was reaching out to him, and yet he continued flailing, trying to save himself, and at the same time, threatening to undo his own rescue.

As a teenager, Gus learned how to lifeguard and knew that saving a drowning person sometimes meant keeping distance lest he take you down with him. Sometimes when saving a drowning person, you must first push him down to get control.

How often those in need of rescue fight those seeking to rescue them and, at times, even cause them to drown. This was a pattern deeply ingrained in Gus' soul. Others had tried to reach out to Gus and offer help. But when struggling, Gus' instinct had been to try to save himself…isolate…keep his distance from others.

"Why do you fight me?" Amy would ask him. "I'm not your enemy. I want to help you. I'm your wife, Gus. I'm not your enemy!"

Yet the self-defense mechanism kicked in at every turn. Even friends from church who'd sought to get to know Gus found themselves stiff-armed. The sad thing was Gus wanted friends. He actually felt the loneliness of not really being known. Yet his gut reaction was to push them away at any chance he got.

This independent, "I don't need you" stuff had a long history for Gus. Though extroverted according to all the personality profile assessments, Gus found himself regularly keeping to himself instead of reaching out to be with people. By turning down chances to be with friends or join other couples for dinner, Gus had started to isolate himself as he got older. That wasn't the way he had been in high school, college, or even in his early twenties, but more and more, Gus kept to himself rather than risk being known—or being rejected.

Instead of moving toward other men and making friends, Gus would sometimes compete with them or compare his level of success to theirs. But Gus had once been glad to let others help him. One time, he and his friend Eddie Armstrong had decided to climb down the back side of Oak Mountain to see whether they could bushwhack their way out from there.

They'd had no idea when they started that they would be free climbing down sheer cliffs with no rope or safety system. At first, the rush of the risk filled both the boys with excitement, but then they came to a place where the rocks started to give out beneath them.

Eddie was below when, suddenly, the rock Gus' left foot was on broke and slid down, barely missing Eddie's face. Then, in an instant, Gus tumbled sideways toward Eddie. Had Eddie not had the presence of mind to extend his hand, Gus would have fallen 100 feet or more to his death. The boys ended up sweating over their near-death experience, but appreciating their bond of friendship and adventure even more.

Gus never climbed down the back of Oak Mountain again.

This time, flailing and practically incoherent in the water, there was no option. He had to allow himself to be rescued.

Like that time on Oak Mountain, the strong hands grabbing Gus didn't quit. Against all of Gus' pushes, clawing, and scratching, the hands surrounded, lifted, and held on.

As Gus looked up at the person pulling him out, he was at once shocked and surprised to see a familiar face. How could this be? Impossible!

Gus found himself staring into the loving eyes of the man he'd loved so much as a boy. It was the man who cared enough to reach out to him in the midst of his pain. The man pulling him from the freezing water was Rodney Turnquest.

CHAPTER 9

WAKING UP

"We're given second chances every day of our life. We don't usually take them, but they're there for the taking."

— Andrew M. Greeley

"**W**hat do you need?" said a calm female voice.

"I...need? I...need?" Gus said barely coherent. "I don't know. What do I need?"

A wonderful aroma—the familiar smell of breakfast—filled Gus' nostrils. Gus breathed deeply to take the sensory memory in. Bacon. Fresh bread. Coffee. That smell mixed a feeling of home and the promise of a new day, not rushed by routine, but enjoyed with family. It was the smell of vacation and seemed to say, "Everything will be okay."

Eyes closed, Gus felt the soothing touch of a hand placed on his.

"We're here for you. We're not going anywhere."

Gus breathed audibly, a relieving sigh. He felt he was surrounded by a palpable presence of love and serenity. But then he remembered. The canoe. The cold water. The cry for help. Was he dead?

"Where am I?" Gus asked.

As Gus opened his eyes, he looked right into the smiling eyes of a beautiful woman staring at him with an almost motherly affection. Her long brown hair hung over Gus, and he felt her calming, peaceful presence. She grinned as she saw his eyes catch hers.

"Well, you're awake! Welcome to Hope!" she said excitedly.

"He's awake!" she announced to the others. Gus heard chairs moving, and he sat up to see a small group of people excitedly moving toward him.

"Well, well, we've been waiting for you!" said one of the men elatedly.

"So he is," said another woman, also moving toward Gus. "We're really, really, glad you're here!" she exclaimed, almost childishly.

"Where am I?" Gus asked.

"You're in Hope," said a young girl in her teens.

"But what about the canoe? I was struggling. I couldn't swim anymore."

"It's okay. We've got you. We're here for you," said another woman,

90

her voice again strangely familiar. As Gus looked at the group surrounding him, he could see he was in a beautiful home... all decked out in Adirondack furniture. Wood chairs, paintings of deer and bears. Most striking was the awesome view out the picture window.

A fire was burning in the fireplace, and Gus could see the mist lifting outside as the early morning sun burnt off the mist.

"Who are you?" Gus asked.

"I'm Mary. And this is Dena, Ethel, Harold, Shelly, and Rodney."

"Am I dead?" Gus asked, surprised to hear himself asking the question—but at the same time, it seemed like a logical question.

"Not quite," said the man introduced as Rodney, smiling. "Last night! Well, almost!"

"Mr. Turnquest?" Gus said puzzled and confused. "Are you Mr. Turnquest? I thought you were dead, but.... What the heck?"

"No need to be swearing, my boy," he said with his prankster grin. Putting his hands on Gus' face, he said, "I'm more alive than ever! But it's you we're concerned about! How are you?"

"Confused. Really, just confused. And I feel like I know everyone else here. Do I know you all?"

"Let's just say we're glad you're back with us," said the younger woman, Shelly. Glancing at the others gathered around, she added, "We all have one common purpose for meeting you in Hope. We believe in you, and we're here to help you get your life back.

Whether you do or not…well, that's still up to you. We've all seen something special in you. Since you were a kid, we have loved you and believed in you.

"Some of these folks felt called to pray for you every day. They put in time for you! But like Mr. Turnquest's letter said, you've been living in the valley of dry bones. You're letting life live you instead of living the life you were born to live. You've heard that *'The future belongs to those who believe in the beauty of their dreams,'* but you don't believe in those dreams anymore. You don't believe in the One who gave you those dreams…well, at least in any measurable way. And we care too much about you to see all of that lost…to you and for what God has been doing in the world," Shelly said.

"Listen to me," said Mr. Turnquest. "Do you want your life back? Would you want to live? Really live? Then we can help you. We now know what life's all about. We'd like you to know as well. To move from the place of dry, dead, and decaying bones into the place of more joy than you could ever imagine. To move from living with borderline depression and continually fighting off despair to actually living with purpose and peace. But the road has to first go through Hope. It starts with Hope. You've already taken the first step by simply saying yes to my letter…even if your motives were a bit mixed! You're here at least."

Then Dena chimed in. "I never gave up on you! And trust me, I was tempted! Even when I was in my nineties, I continued to pray for you. I said, 'God, do you want me to continue praying for that boy?' And God said, 'Dena, you don't give up! You keep praying for him! He needs you!'"

As she said those words, Gus recognized her: "Mrs. Daniels! This is incredible! But, how old are you? Excuse me for asking?"

"Well, a girl doesn't like to give away her age, now, Gus; you know that," said Dena Daniels with a grin.

"But, but, you must be...."

"Would you like to join us for some fresh bread and homemade breakfast?" asked Mary, interrupting the age discussion.

Smelling the scent emanating from the kitchen, there was no way Gus couldn't. Besides, he was starting to feel hungry, and the aroma was out of this world.

"We're going to eat on the deck," said the man named Ed. He offered his hand, pulled Gus up, and led him to a table, which was set in perfect Adirondack style.

The table was filled with beautiful linens, perfectly suited China plates, and then surrounded by fresh strawberries, blueberries, and even fresh flowers in the middle. The deck overlooked the lake with the ripples of small waves glistening in the morning sun. A gentle breeze stirred the colored leaves on the trees and the sound of a wind chime could be heard nearby.

"If I'm dead," thought Gus, "then heaven sure seems to be a lot like the Adirondacks." As a kid, he had actually wondered how heaven could be more beautiful than those mountains. The scene in front of him was certainly about as beautiful as he had ever seen.

Everyone took a seat around the table. At that point, Mr. Turnquest was handed a loaf of homemade whole wheat bread, some eggs, and incredible maple syrup dipped bacon. The aroma caught on the gentle breeze, drifting past Gus and bringing him back to better days with his own family in the Adirondacks.

After asking everyone to grab hands for a prayer, Mr. Turnquest said a blessing and the food was passed. Gus filled his plate as if he hadn't eaten in a long time. Everything looked and smelled of home.

"The Resistance did not want you here, my friend," said Mr. Turnquest. "The Resistance doesn't want you to know what you are about to learn. Instead, the Resistance wants people like you stuck. It wants you depressed. Wants you to bury your dreams. Wants you to live isolated. Alone. Not dead, but as good as.

"You're engaged in the struggle taking place all around us. A war. It's a struggle for good to triumph over evil. A struggle for beauty to triumph over ugliness. A struggle for love to triumph over apathy. For your God-given purpose to triumph over darkness. That's the history of the world. You have been chosen and given a mission that's unique to you. You've been given a bigger purpose…and you must not fail to fulfill it."

Mr. Turnquest's deep blue eyes pierced into Gus' very soul. He lifted bread, gave thanks, broke it, and began to give pieces to everyone at the table.

Then, again, looking directly into Gus' eyes, he said, "You've come to Hope for a reason. That's why you didn't drown last night."

CHAPTER 10

ENCOUNTERING HOPE

"The thing is to understand myself, to see what God really wants
me to do; the thing is to find a truth which is true for me, to find
the idea for which I can live or die."

— Soren Kierkegaard

"**O**kay, I've got to say, Mr. T," said Gus, "those
were about the nicest people I've ever met.
And they all seem to know me or believe
something about me. It's kind of wonderful,
yet creepy. These people pray for me every day! What are you folks?
Angels or something?"

"Ha! I love that! Wonderful, yet creepy! Angels! No. Not hardly.
Yet, I agree; Hope's no ordinary place, Gus," said Mr. Turnquest,
looking him in the eye with an intensity that felt both challenging
and inviting.

"I feel like I've just gone down some kind of wormhole and ended up in Narnia or somewhere! Like this can't be for real," Gus said.

"Why can't it?" asked Mr. Turnquest.

"Because you're all just so nice! Actually, that's not the right word. Present, maybe. Caring. You all seem to be so happy. So excited about me and about each other. And you all possess some kind of hard-to-fathom belief that there's something special or important about me! Like I'm some chosen person or something."

"Let's take a walk, Gus," said Mr. Turnquest, "I want you to see something that I, frankly, think is really messed up!"

Mr. Turnquest lent Gus a light jacket and some dry hiking boots, and then the two walked out the front door and headed toward the lake. As Gus looked back at the house, he was awed by its rustic beauty.

It was three stories, with wraparound porches at almost every level. Wood beams, green panel, at least three stone fireplaces, and large windows all over. It mixed dark wood and light wood masterfully. Out front was a dock with at least three boats. It was the most beautiful house Gus had ever seen—rustic elegance were the words that came to mind. Not opulent. But beautiful.

The two men walked up the long gravel driveway and took a right, heading down the road. Once again, the magic of the autumn leaves in full array startled Gus—greens and yellows, light reds and deep burgundy—all glimmering in the morning sun.

"I get that sense," said Gus. "You all seem to have some bigger view of life. Like talk of things like purpose and destiny. You talk as if you know there's some kind of Resistance out there trying to shut me down or stop me. I don't think I'm that deep or see things like you."

"I'd like to take you to what was once the richest place in Hope. Would you like to see that?" Mr. Turnquest asked.

"Sure," said Gus. "From the look of your house and some of the others I see around this town, this place has money. It's not the Hope I remember. It doesn't even seem like the same town I saw yesterday! It's the same awesome landscape, but it seems more alive. The people are more alive! And this may sound strange, but it seems like you can see the economy booming…it seems like there's more money here than I've seen in any town in this part of the state!"

"Well, this place is special," said Mr. Turnquest.

As they passed others on the road—some out for runs, some riding four wheelers, others in jeeps—every single person waved, smiled, and gave a hearty greeting to Rodney Turnquest, as if he were their very best friend.

"Hey, Rodney! How's it going, my brothah?" shouted one younger man.

And opposed to what Gus remembered Adirondack towns being like, Gus noted a blend of races: Asian, Hispanic, White, and African-American. Gus saw a diverse group working together to fix a fence. Others were chatting down by the lake, just seeming to enjoy each other's company. He could hear roaring laughter coming from a group of women standing nearby.

Mr. Turnquest began pointing out buildings...all with a rustic elegance. They weren't pretentious, but they were all designed to fit into the beauty of the natural surroundings.

"That's the entrepreneur training academy, Gus," said Mr. Turnquest, pointing to a building that looked like a classic Adirondack lodge. "And that's the Hope School for the Creative Arts. And that building down by the lake is the new Center for Environmental Preservation."

"Sure not quite the Hope I remember from earlier years, Mr. T," said Gus, looking around at all the new construction in town. It was all in the classic Adirondack style, but downtown Hope had a string of new restaurants, art stores, a flower shop, spa, health club, some new churches, a cheese shop, and a few new specialty stores.

"Great taste and not overdone," Gus said. "But from what I recall, Hope was more of a one general store and a gaudy pizza parlor place. Looks like the economy sure has changed!"

"Yeah, there's definitely some entrepreneurship and creative growth going on," said Mr. Turnquest. "We're all about unleashing creativity and business is booming. Believe it or not, some smart folks quit working in the city and brought some high tech start-ups right here to Hope. And a lot of them work from home—that is when they're not fishing or skiing or having fun out on party boats. We work hard, pray hard, and play hard!

Property values are going through the roof, and there's plenty of construction, within limits, of course. Also, there's a boom in updating classic homes. And a lot of people in Hope are involved in overseas projects."

"What kinds of overseas projects?" asked Gus.

"Well, we realize that with our ability to communicate and use the Internet, we can create jobs and solve problems in places on the other side of the globe. We call the movement 'Entrepreneur on Purpose.' Its goal is to empower the incredible people right here in Hope to be able to start businesses, non-profits, educational programs, or whatever to meet needs and solve problems all over the planet."

"From the Adirondacks?" said Gus in disbelief.

"Why not? God's natural beauty inspires our best creative thinking! And we're not in a rush, like in the big city hustle and bustle. We have Wi-Fi here you know, Gus! And the airport's just a hop, skip, and a jump away. We discovered the trend where more and more people could free up their time and life by creating businesses, products, or services around the value they could offer.

"Ever see those signs, 'If you lived here, you'd be home right now!'"

"Sure," said Gus.

"Well, we created one that says 'Hope: If you worked here, you'd be at work right now!' And we're convinced the rugged beauty and opportunity to be out in nature creates a much better work environment. Would you rather work here or in some cubicle in some crowded downtown?

"Gus, life in Hope's a dream for me! And for everyone else who lives here! Hope has more millionaires per capita than any town in America. And if you've noticed, people here live to a ripe old age, and still remain healthy and engaged in our community and beyond. But part of the beauty of it is that's not what makes the town so rich."

"What makes it so rich, then?"

"I'll show you," said Mr. Turnquest.

Gus and Mr. Turnquest rounded the corner and came to an iron gate on the left side of the road with "Hope Cemetery" engraved in gold above it.

"You're taking me in here? The cemetery?" Gus said, somewhat surprised and feeling somewhat tricked. "From what you're describing, I hardly believe people around here die much!"

"Not as much or as young as they used to. But, yep, we haven't solved the live forever thing. God pretty much holds that secret close to the vest. But Gus, this cemetery used to be the richest place in Hope! Used to be, Gus. It's not anymore. As you can see, things are different around here now," Mr. Turnquest said.

The two walked into the cemetery. Gus could see headstones dating back to the 1800s, their names and dates weathered by the years and the Adirondack winters. Mixed in with those were stones from the 1900s, and even some that were clearly recent additions.

"Gus, I used to think the richest places around were gold mines and diamond mines—banks filled with cash. But for most towns, cities, and nations on earth, the richest places are the graveyards. It used to be that way in Hope, too. But that's different now.

"For generations, the cemetery snatched our gifted people, claiming really good people whose big dreams were never fulfilled—their bigger purpose never expressed. Inventions never created. Businesses never started. Relationships never built or rebuilt. Visions never identified. Without much hope that they'd succeed, most just give up on dreams. They don't think the risk will pan out. They don't have the energy or the motivation to pursue their goals. So they don't!

"Hope was hardly a blip on anyone's radar, Gus. It was a little hamlet with barely 400 people. Many were unemployed or at least underemployed. Sure, there were summer folks who flocked here from the city and had houses on the lake. But the townies kind of held them in contempt—saw them taking from Hope, but not giving much back. Well, maybe some taxes!

"A good number of the families here were fractured. Single moms. Marriages in shambles. Alcoholism was pretty much a way of coping. There certainly weren't great amounts of creative industry or entrepreneurship. Good people, no doubt. But not any real vision or creative spirit. And so the riches of Hope ended up in the graveyard. Year after year, good people ended up here with their dreams still inside them. People with artistic gifts didn't do art. People with skills to organize didn't bother. People with the ability to help other people pretty much kept to themselves.

"The thing is, most didn't see Hope as being very different from other towns in this country. It certainly had enough natural beauty to hide what was really going on in the culture.

"Folks in Hope believed in heaven, Gus. They believed there was a better life when they died. But they didn't see the point in desiring much more for themselves here. Some went to church, but *went* was the extent of it. It didn't seem to apply much to everyday life. We celebrated holidays. But people would joke—ain't much hope in Hope!

"Read that one, Gus," Mr. Turnquest said, directing Gus over to one of the headstones.

Gus walked over to the stone.

"What does it say, Gus?"

"It says Rodney Turnquest! What? How can that be? Mr. T, are you dead?"

"Ha!" Mr. Turnquest burst out with another hearty laugh. "No, Gus. I'm right here, aren't I? Feeling pretty healthy too! But I might as well have been dead. I spent, actually wasted, many years of my life not doing the things I loved most. Once I discovered hope, I actually had this created to remind me that I had almost wasted my life…and that the years I still have are a gift.

"Now read what's written on the back of the stone, Gus."

Gus moved around behind the gravestone and bent over to read the longer inscription.

> "For the secret of man's being is not only to live…but to live for something definite. Without a firm notion of what he is living for, man will not accept life and will rather destroy himself than remain on earth…."
>
> — Fyodor Dostoevsky

"Wow! Interesting quote, Mr. T. But why? Why's that there?" Gus asked.

"That right there is what makes Hope, Hope, Gus."

"What do you mean?" asked Gus, still puzzled by this whole experience. "A quote from a dead Russian writer?"

"Ha!" again Mr. Turnquest laughed. "No. Finding what we in Hope were meant to do. Finding and unleashing our bigger purpose. Discovering and experiencing the kind of hope that could change things. Sharing that hope with the world. What does that say to you, Gus?"

"Live for something definite, not just live?" Gus said. "It sounds good. Maybe kind of lofty and unattainable when your life's pretty screwed up. Like, sure, I'm glad you think about bigger things like Dostoevsky did, but right now, I'm just overwhelmed trying to keep my life, my marriage, and my kids afloat.

"Mr. T, I appreciate you wanting to guide me to some higher purpose you all think I have. But at this point, I just don't have it in me to consider how things could be different. Sure! I'd love to have something definite, but I guess I'm more in the destroy myself part of this.

"I know you've always been kind of happy and positive, Mr. T, but that's just not the way I am," added Gus. "And the people in Hope— it's great they're all so nice and fulfilled, but that's not what people are like where I'm from."

As Gus finished his sentence, the two were suddenly interrupted by a distressed voice.

"Rodney! Hey, have you heard what's going on? A 10-100 down by the lake!"

"Gus, this is Pete Sidney, our local sheriff," said Mr. Turnquest. After Gus and Pete shook hands, Mr. Turnquest said, "What's that again, Pete? I'm a little rusty on my police codes. What's a 10-100?"

"A coroner case, Rodney. A couple of fisherman just found a body in the weeds on the side of the lake. A man. Looks to be middle-aged. Caucasian. Found him washed up on the side of the lake in some tall grass. "Looks like a victim of drowning," said Pete. "A huge gash on the side of his head like he'd been whacked somehow."

"Oh, man! God bless his soul," said Mr. Turnquest, instantly offering up a prayer. "Any idea who he is? Anyone reported missing?"

"No one. No one's got a clue who this guy is. Fresh case, though. Doesn't seem to have been down there long."

CHAPTER 11

MR. TURNQUEST'S STORY

"Now, with God's help, I shall become myself."

— Soren Kierkegaard

In another minute, Gus, Mr. Turnquest, and Sheriff Sidney were walking down toward the lake. From a few hundred yards, they could see four men carrying a stretcher with a white sheet covering what was clearly a lifeless body.

Red ambulance lights beamed.

"It's just so strange," Pete Sidney said.

"What's that?" Mr. Turnquest asked.

"Strange that someone around here would be all alone out on the lake—fully dressed. No one knows where he came from."

"Yeah, that is kind of odd," Mr. Turnquest said. "Do you need me for anything, Pete?"

"I'm fine. Team of volunteers all showed up to help out."

"Okay, I'm around if you need me, Pete. Don't hesitate to involve me."

"You know I won't, Rodney," the sheriff said as he walked off toward where the group of volunteer paramedics was still huddled.

Once back at his house, Mr. Turnquest poured some homemade lemonade for Gus and himself. They stood around the huge granite island in Mr. Turnquest's awesomely equipped kitchen, light beaming in from large skylights.

"Gus, I want to come back to something you said that wasn't true."

"What's that?" asked Gus.

"You said, 'I know you've always been kind of happy and positive.'"

"Well," said Gus, "that's why I think you may not fully understand my struggle. You've always been so upbeat and positive. Things just seem to work for you."

"Ha!" Mr. Turnquest exclaimed.

"Why do you say 'Ha'?" Gus asked.

"Well, Partner, I guess I'm glad that's what you see. But I've been through the muck and mire, and I know more pain, darkness, and gloom than you might imagine. In fact, hold on a minute—let me grab something. I'll be right back."

Mr. Turnquest disappeared for a minute and returned carrying a well-worn, leather-bound book…or maybe it was a journal. Gus was not sure.

Mr. Turnquest flipped through it. He found the page he was looking for and started reading.

> I can no longer see any future or answers for my life. The lights have all gone out and I'm stuck in mire that goes on without end.
>
> No, I'm drowning in black tar. The black tar is all around. I can't breathe. I can't see. No more color. No oxygen.
>
> I take deep breaths, but only sighs come out.
>
> I feel like a ghost. No longer part of a real, physical world. I hear voices and see people, but they're just far away. They have no idea there's a drowning person in their midst. They could not care less. They seem to be breathing even though I'm not.
>
> I feel worthless and numb. Like the perpetual sadness won't leave. Can't leave. My confidence has left me. I don't have the energy any more to love or to feel like I can accept anyone's love. My sadness has enveloped me and it has won.
>
> I can't get out of my own way and don't even want to. Simple tasks, putting away my own dishes or making my bed…I can't do.

The rest of the world has no idea what's happening and they wouldn't care. I just don't matter. Why should I?

The things I used to enjoy no longer make me happy. Spring. No. Food. No. Watching movies. Sports. Reading. Everything just seems to take too much energy. I've lost all desire to celebrate. Christmas feels like a jolly farce. So does church. People in church—I loathe their empty and shallow smiles. Even worse is when I force my own smile. I want to get sick right in front of them.

I can't sleep. I wake up and lie there, tortured. Then in the day, I want to do nothing but sleep, since at least when I'm asleep, I don't have to think.

Someone has turned out the light inside me, and now I'm forced to live in this darkness. This loneliness. This hell.

There's just no escape. No hope. Nothing, but nothing. I am nothing. Stuck here in this nothing. Dead. Dying. No. Dead.

Mr. Turnquest lowered the journal. Tears formed in his eyes. He looked up at Gus.

"What do you think?" he asked.

"Really, really sad. Really sad. That person gets it. Really gets it. I think I could have said many of those words. That person just said it better. Whose words are those?" Gus asked.

"Partner, those would be my words. This is my journal from some years ago. I lived in that dungeon for years. No one…no one would have thought that I struggled this deeply. My business card said I was the president of a company. I lived in a fabulous house in an upscale town. People would have thought I was doing just fine. I let them think that.

"I wasn't."

"I had no idea," said Gus. "Absolutely no idea! I just figured you were some kind of born optimist or just naturally happy or something. A guy of great faith."

"Gus, I'm incredibly happy now. I have faith, and I'm very much an optimist…now. But that was before the Habits of Hope. That was before I learned about and started practicing the strategies of self-leadership.

"As you can tell, I was in a dark place. A very, very dark place. I thought I would never escape. That there was no escape. At least for me."

"That's hard to believe! Those words seem so out of place coming from you, Mr. T. In fact, I'm speechless. That sounds a whole lot more like me."

"Gus, I was in that valley of dry bones, and I thought my life was pretty much over. In fact, it almost was. I was all about leading everyone else and even building businesses. However, I struggled to lead the most important person. Me! I felt kind of like an empty shell. I thought my best years were behind me."

"What in the world triggered you to get to such a low point, Mr. T? Did something really bad happen? Did someone die?"

"You know, you'd think that would be the case. Frankly, it was chronic disappointment. I felt like a fraud. I felt like my work was sucking me dry. The struggle of making a living but having no life—nothing beyond taking care of me and mine. But, like the writer in Ecclesiastes put it, 'Meaningless, meaningless! Everything is meaningless!' I lacked any bigger purpose. At least that I knew of."

"I still find that so hard to believe," said Gus.

"Gus, after years of my unknowing self-preoccupation, I had lousy relationships with Alice and the kids. Hardly anyone could tell. I did all the small talk and attended the parties. But at the end of every night, I just felt alone. Deeply alone. And I lacked any real friendships. Especially other guys. I was making money. But to tell you the truth, I was much better at making it than keeping it.

"Gus, spend enough time feeling sorry for yourself and feeling like a failure and your inner light starts to grow dim. Self-pity is really the most destructive form of drug, and I was a regular user. Practically all the sadness most of us experience in life comes from feeling sorry for ourselves. But who knew?

"I was lost, Partner. Looking so good to the outside world, yet lost. And I had no excuse for myself. I had dug my own hole. And that hole was empty, lonely, and dark."

"So what was missing for you?" Gus asked, still shocked at what he was hearing.

"What wasn't missing, Partner? I was seeing money as a drug and our finances were a mess. My marriage was on the rocks. Alice let me know I was a mess as a husband. Our sex life was basically non-existent. And I couldn't convince her I was great. But, in reality, there was nothing bigger than me. I can now see in the rearview mirror. It was all about me. *All* about me!

"The day I wrote that journal entry was just about as deep as it got. By that time, Alice was threatening to leave me. Sarah was flunking out of school and getting involved with some creepy guys. Ron was in trouble with the police for using and selling drugs. I could hardly get out of bed in the morning, and I'd been struggling to make sales for over two years. I hated my job. I loathed the people I worked with. I couldn't stand selling a product I didn't care about, didn't believe in, and would never have used myself. I was broken. Desperate. Drowning. But I didn't see anyone who could rescue me or even throw me a float.

"And to make matters worse, that day my doctor told me if I didn't change my habits, cut the drinking, and start exercising, I was going to die young. I hated the me I saw in the mirror, but I just kept eating junk, drinking to calm my nerves, and letting exercise become something I had done when I was a kid in gym class.

"And you see, I was beating up on the only person I could legally beat up. Me. Myself. I beat myself with voices. I hated me! I'd call myself 'idiot,' 'jackass,' 'failure,' 'loser.' I won't repeat some of the other terms I used. And where else could I go with my disappointment? I couldn't whine to anyone but myself, really.

"Oh, I whined to Alice sometimes, and I told her how much I hated my life, but she didn't get it. And telling her how crappy things were for me only seemed to drive us further and further apart. I just thought I was being honest about how I really was. I didn't know I was instilling fear and negativity in her and making her afraid to get near me. She'd say, 'I have to walk on eggshells around you or you'll explode again about how lousy your life is!'

"When Alice died, I felt like my behavior had cut her life short—like the years of stress had damaged her immune system. No one would have known or accused me, but I knew."

"So how did things change, Mr. T? Clearly, you're not stuck anymore. In fact, what I'm seeing right now in Hope is the absolute opposite of how desperate you were back then. Your kids love you! You're surrounded by more friends than I've ever seen one man, especially a man, have! How did you get from living in hell to living in such hope and happiness?"

"Do you really want to know?" Mr. Turnquest asked.

"Of course!" said Gus.

"No, I mean do you really want to know? I'm not talking about simple answers. I'm talking about dynamite. I can share the real deal. But I'll only share this if you are open to a way of life that changes *everything*!

"What changed everything for me—what took a hopeless mess and brought me to a place of wanting others to experience what I've experienced, and in the years since has transformed a town named Hope into a place filled with hope—was being given a gift that brought purpose to the dead me. I was given strategies that led to the life most people want…but just have no roadmap so they can find it! It's what makes Hope the richest place on earth. Not the graveyard!

"In fact, it's going to be like sharing the secret of the city of Eldorado's gold or giving you a GPS with Atlantis' coordinates."

"Wow! So this is a big deal, huh?" Gus said.

"Bigger deal. Big deal's an understatement, Gus! What I have learned about hope actually changes everything. What I've learned transforms those at their wits end or can empower people who are just underperforming a bit. It can create cultures of leadership and hope in companies. And it can change whole families, communities, and churches. In fact, Partner, if you're open to it, I'll share the secrets of what makes Hope, Hope."

"Wow! That significant, huh?" said Gus.

"That significant. But I'll only share these with a big if…if you will at least consider making this your own way of life. If that's of no interest, then I'd rather just share the general concepts or not share at all. You see, if you're not open to taking them to heart, they'll just be some old concepts that work for Mr. T but have no relevance for you.

"These Habits of Hope make Hope the richest place on earth. Actually, a slice of heaven on earth. But only some people are ready for it. Most are not ready," Mr. Turnquest said.

"How do you know when you're ready?" Gus asked.

"You're ready when you're sick and tired of just getting by and you're ready to go to work on the biggest project you can," Mr. Turnquest said.

"What project is that?"

"The You-Project. Your life. Your leadership. Your freedom. What do you think?" Mr. Turnquest asked. "Do you want to know the Habits of Hope?"

"Mr. T, why not? Heck, you saved me from drowning! And frankly, I have a sense there's something bigger out there for me. I've just never really known where to start. Actually, I didn't want to hope things could be different! Especially if there was no path!"

"Well, then let's take that path. But let's do it together. If you trust me, I'll share the strategy that leads to the life you've always wanted…. Even if you thought it might not exist.

"And we're gonna start this journey with a little tour," Mr. Turnquest smirked.

"What do you mean 'a little tour'?" Gus asked.

"Actually a tour through some places you may find quite familiar. If you're open to it, I'll take you on the same journey I went on… the journey everyone in Hope has gone on."

"Okay," Gus said, now silently wondering what he might have signed up for.

"But before I share the Habits of Hope, I want to introduce you to the *why* behind it. Gus, until you have a big enough 'Why,' no what or how is going to make any difference. The power of the Habits are in the 'Why.'

"It's a question you should be asking before embarking on this journey. It's what I asked! Without asking and answering this question, sharing the Habits of Hope is a waste of time."

CHAPTER 12

SICK OF THE STATUS QUO

"Too many of us are not living our dreams
because we are living our fears."

— Les Brown

When you're surrounded by the constant beauty of the Adirondacks, it's sometimes hard to recognize the inner struggles of the people you meet. In some ways, the people of the region are proud of their ability to keep their challenges to themselves. It's almost as if the harsh winter months enable them to develop a thicker skin than people in other parts of the country.

"As a kid I was a big fan of Popeye the Sailor Man. Did you ever see that cartoon, Partner?" Mr. Turnquest asked, looking out at the mountains from his favorite living room chair.

"Oh, sure. Reruns galore! 'Hey, Olive, get me, me spinach,'" Gus said in his best Popeye accent.

"Not bad! But do remember what happened when he couldn't take it any longer. Chained up…his girlfriend captive, Bluto basically taking over…even laughing at his weakness. Then he would pop a can of 'me spinach' and shout, 'That's all I can stands, 'cause I canst stands no more!' Then he'd go Popeye on Bluto!"

"Yep. Love that!" Gus said.

"Well, that's where things start. Change won't happen if you don't see a problem you're tired of. As long as you're okay with the mess you're in, you won't ask and seek out anything better.

"It reminds me of seeing a guy stuck in a snowbank last winter. I drove by and he was clearly stuck—spinning his wheels. No traction. Nothing but ice and snow. Stuck. I pulled over and rolled down my window. I said, 'Hey, pal! Can I help you? At least I can push.' You know what he did? He said, 'Nah, I'll get it. I'm good.'

"'You sure?' I asked. He just waved.

"Later that night, I drove by again. Sure enough. Still stuck. For some reason, that guy just couldn't acknowledge he was stuck and needed a way out. Not sure what his deal was! Almost all of us get stuck at some point. We lose hope. If we just settle for stuck, we stay stuck. When we settle for something less than fully alive, we're pretty much settling for defeat. When defeat gets inside our souls, it starts to move out the good and grows like a nasty cancer. It works its way up to our eyes and fogs the lenses. We start seeing life through this foggy lens and begin to think that's just how life looks! Hopeless is as hopeless does.

"There are three key realizations that need to take place for hope to return," Mr. Turnquest went on.

"*First*: I'm stuck! Didn't intend to get stuck. Don't like that I'm stuck! But the truth is I'm not fully alive! I'm not thriving. I'm not taking life by the neck and being fully there!

"*Second*: I am not going to settle for stuck. I see others who aren't stuck driving by me. I can be moving a whole lot better. This doesn't have to take forever. I just need to change.

"*Third*: I will take action! I will find answers. I will overcome whatever got me here and do something about it. 'That's all I can stands 'cause I canst stands no more!'

"Too many accept awful as a way of life when an audacious life is what awaits!"

"Mr. T, how did you get stuck? Or lose hope?" Gus asked.

How Rodney Turnquest Got Stuck

"I not only got stuck in the town of Hopeless. I became its mayor!" Mr. Turnquest replied.

"I realize some people get stuck from something traumatic that rocks their soul—lose a loved one, get sick. I had a friend whose son took his own life. Hard not to get stuck when something like that happens! At least for a time.

"I think it started for me when I realized just how much I hated my job. I'd gone to college for it, of course, with no idea that it wasn't a fit for me at all. I figured this out after being in the profession for years. I just started to realize that every time Sunday came, I got a nasty pit in my stomach. I became short with Alice. I couldn't stand the thought of another week of the crap my boss slung. His tantrums over the dumbest things. The way people talked behind each other's backs. The sense that all that mattered was making the numbers.

"I asked, 'Is it possible to be fulfilled in work?' But I realized that asking only made me more and more unhappy! I was a pretty young guy, but I was counting the days until my next vacation and the years until I could retire!"

"I so identify!" interrupted Gus. "Why is it I feel like you've been reading my mind? I feel like I try to tell myself my work is just my work. My job. My paycheck. But it doesn't seem to do it!"

"Because we were created for meaningful work, Gus! The first thing God did after creating human beings was to provide them with work. It's right from Genesis 1:28:

"God blessed them and said to them, *'Be fruitful and increase in number; fill the earth and subdue it. Rule over the fish in the sea and the birds in the sky and over every living creature that moves on the ground.'*

"So how do you think it's affecting so many of us who don't feel like work is meaningful? We end up feeling disengaged. Bored. Frustrated. It's not meant to be that way, Gus. But that affects everything else. Or at least it can. It did for me!

"That just started me down the road of seeing myself as one of the cursed ones in life. I'll get to how to change that soon, but let me just say, I began to rehearse in my mind all the ways life sucked.

How I was trapped. How 'life's tough, then you die.' Nasty. Brutish. Short! So, what the heck?

"And let me just say, the mind has a way of agreeing with us! It begins to send signals to the rest of the body that say, 'Heads up! Life sucks!' And it's like the body looks for quick fix ways out! For me, it was my sweet tooth and love of eating junk. Candy bars for lunch. Donuts. Cake. Ice cream. Coffee all day long, not to mention happy hours after work to relax. Felt like I deserved it! It's like the dominoes begin to fall. Soon I didn't feel like I had it in me to play basketball or work out. I stopped hitting the trails to walk or get outside. Didn't have time for hobbies or volunteering. Church? Only on holidays.

"I just didn't like myself! And when we don't like ourselves, guess how others start to feel about us? It's like they pick up on the signals we're sending! I fought with Alice all the time. I was short with her and felt like she wasn't much fun to be around. Not that I was, you understand. But it's like she had this snarl on her face whenever I was home. She called me the dark vortex, and I told her, 'Thanks, Miss Perfect!'"

"Wow!" Gus said. "It's pretty hard for me to imagine you like that. I thought you were always optimistic and successful."

"It's hard to believe I let *me* get to that place. But you're either busy living or busy dying. Partner, I was awful busy dying…just stretching it out some."

"Did you ever think of taking your life?" Gus asked.

"Well, you know, never had a plan to…. But when you can't sleep at night, your job feels like a jail, and your marriage feels like a prison, so you start to wonder."

"I know God is really important to you, Mr. T. Where was God during that time for you?"

"Ever heard of the Dark Night of the Soul, Partner?"

"Not sure."

"Well, let's just say, I didn't sense or feel much God at the time. The dark night of the soul was a term used by the Catholic mystic St. John of the Cross to describe a period when you don't sense the good things of God or feel God's presence in any real way. In *The Crack-Up*, F. Scott Fitzgerald said, "In a real dark night of the soul it is always three o'clock in the morning." That was when it tended to hit me. Actually, mine was closer to beginning at two!"

"What did you do?" Gus asked.

Masking Stuckness

"Well, you know the desire is for a quick fix. Feed the mind and dull the pain. Pretty much what today's anti-depressants are all about. Clearly, there are medically-necessary times to adjust chemicals gone haywire in the brain. And I don't have any problem with those…for a time. The key is 'for a time.' Not as a way of life!" Mr. Turnquest said.

"But in a world where more than one in ten people regularly take antidepressants, you've got to think that doctors have pretty much begun thinking that loss of hope is treatable in the same way you'd treat a cold. Prescribe something until it goes away! No!

"The rate of antidepressant use has skyrocketed nearly 400 percent in the United States since the late 1980s when they went on the market. There's lots of evidence that the rates of depression have doubled from the late 1990s to the late 2000s. Is it the chicken or the egg?"

"Outside of Hope, it sure doesn't seem to be getting better. Do you think there's a better way?" Gus asked. "I've got to believe there is. I just couldn't think of how to help others! Mostly because I couldn't figure out how to help me! So you've got my attention. I never would have imagined you'd been through all this!"

"As the Englishman G.K. Chesterton said, '*There are many, many angles at which one can fall, but only one angle at which one can stand straight.*' And I found every angle there was to lean! I drank. I ate carbohydrates and sweets. I slept instead of thinking about things. And my performance at work just got worse and worse. Something had to change. I just had no clue how to change. Actually, change seemed either impossible or it required more energy than I had.

Do You Want to Change? Ask.

"I always believe change is impossible for those who won't take one simple step. And to tell you the truth, I don't think most people have done this—*yet*. *Yet* is the key word."

Mr. Turnquest paused and just stood, still staring at Gus.

Gus stared back in the silence.

Finally, Gus broke the silence. "They haven't done what? What won't they do?"

"Ask."

"Ask?" said Gus, thinking Mr. Turnquest's answer was far too simple for the plague of problems he had just described.

"'Ask and you will receive. Seek and you will find.' That's what the Good Book says. One day I was sitting on top of Panther Mountain, just staring out into the hills. I was wondering what was next. I had pretty much come to the end of it and was sick of my life as it was. You may say I'm crazy, but I know I heard the voice of God. Or an angel. Or something. I heard '*Ask*.' And like you, my question was '*Ask what*?'

"'Ask' I heard again. 'Ask what?' 'Ask for hope.'"

"Wow!" said Gus, kind of surprised. "Then what?"

"That was it. But in that moment, even while I was still confused, I felt like I wasn't alone. I had a first step. A simple, doable first step out of my stuck-ness."

"What happened next?" asked Gus, now wondering whether Mr. Turnquest wasn't a bit more whacky than he had first thought.

"That was the beginning of the greatest adventure of my life and the greatest breakthroughs I've ever experienced. Asking changed everything. Somehow on that mountain that day, God heard my prayer. *Ask*. It was the beginning of everything! I grabbed a pen and a piece of paper and began to write words that answered the questions: 'What do I do if I've lost hope? How do I get it back?'

"At first, they didn't make much sense. But as I looked out over the

Adirondack vista from Panther Mountain, I began to realize these were no ordinary words. They were a revelation. They were a way out."

"Wow!" said Gus. "So you seemed to think they were God's way of helping you get unstuck."

"At first, I wasn't positive that was the case. Now I have no question. When you recognize you've been given a way to peace, to purpose, and to relevant hope, you just know. 'Ask and you will receive,' Gus. That's what I did. 'Seek and you will find.' Of course, that's a spiritual act of faith. But we are spiritual people living in a spiritual world. And God's plan for your life is always better than ours! So why not ask? That's the kind of prayer God loves to answer. God, we all desperately need hope! Hope changes everything. And by everything, I mean everything!"

"Mr. T, I've got to believe this whole weird experience—the letter, the trip to Hope, almost drowning, reconnecting with you— happened for a reason. I'm in no place to think this is all a big coincidence.

"And frankly, for me to just keep doing the same things expecting different results when I go home feels like an invitation back into a trap. But you seem so convinced that *hope* is the key to changing everything. I'm still not convinced. Or maybe I don't know what the kind of hope you're describing really is. How would experiencing hope affect my job? My marriage? My own sense of purposelessness?"

"Gus, are you open to doing the first thing?"

129

"Which first thing?"

"What I just shared—ask. Ask God for help. It's the humbling recognition of two things. One: there is a God. Two: you're not God."

"Sure. What do I have to lose?" Gus asked.

"Well, just being God, I guess. Or at least a god!" said Mr. Turnquest, with a smile.

"Well, me being God certainly isn't working. I'm open," Gus said.

"Just say it."

"Out loud?" questioned Gus.

"Yeah."

"That feels awkward!"

"Yep. So ask," Mr. Turnquest said.

"God, I need hope. Whatever it looks like. I'm in. Can I have it?" Gus asked.

"The journey begins!" Mr. Turnquest said with a beaming smile.

CHAPTER 13

HOPE CHANGES EVERYTHING

"Hope changes everything. It changes winter into summer, darkness into dawn, descent into ascent, barrenness into creativity, agony into joy. Hope is the sun. It is light. It is passion. It is the fundamental force for life's blossoming."

— Daisaku Ikeda

"Somehow," said Mr. Turnquest, continuing his discussion with Gus, "so many of us get it into our brains that we can't change. Things can't change. We feel like it's as good as it's gonna get, or even worse, it's gonna get nothing but worse. We'll never be as young. Never be as smart. Never be wanted."

"Why hope, Mr. T? Why do you see that as so vital?" asked Gus.

"I could go on and on here, but, briefly, hope's the very foundation of almost everything good in our lives. Outside of love, hope's the most powerful attribute you can possess.

"Think about it, Gus…

"Hope's the foundation of faith, enabling us to believe in possibility.

"Hope's the path to a positive imagination.

"Hope's the only lasting antidote for depression.

"Hope's the way to start winning when you've become too used to losing.

"Hope's the solution to suicide.

"Hope's the way forward when you're stuck and settling for a poor excuse of a life.

"Gus, hope is the key to your future. But you've got to know how to attain it!"

"Hope, at its core, is having a positive imagination. By imagination, I'm not talking about thinking of fairies and green dragons as if they exist. A positive imagination is about having the ability to form a powerful picture in your mind of something you haven't seen or experienced. It's a skill. And with hope, you anticipate that what you imagine and desire will happen. You picture good things coming into reality. You envision a brighter tomorrow and see it fulfilled."

"Makes total sense," said Gus. "But what happens when hope's not present?"

"The lack of hope deflates your soul. If you don't believe you've got a future worth striving for, you'll start quitting…one moment, one decision, one dream deferred at a time. When your spirit loses hope, you don't have faith to believe that what isn't happening *now* can ever happen *then*.

"Discouragement and despair tells those who've had a dream that, 'If it hasn't happened by now, it will never happen!' Our souls just weren't designed to live without hope. Hopelessness is toxic to our souls.

"Hope says just the opposite. It says your goals can still be achieved. You can still do it. Better days are ahead, not behind. One of my absolute favorite passages in the Bible is in the book of Jeremiah. God tells a bunch of disheartened people, *'For I know the plans I have for you, declares the Lord, plans for welfare and not for evil, to give you a future and a hope.'* (Jeremiah 29:11)

"That speaks to me too, Mr. T," said Gus. "Do you think that applies to people today?"

"Gus, it's God's very nature to want to give heart back to those who've lost heart. That verse says God can see the future and has a plan for the best possible outcome.

"Gus, were you in the military? Or did you play a team sport?"

"Not in the military. I played football, basketball, some baseball."

"Okay, then you'll get this. One of the most significant things any team or squad can have is the belief that they can win or pull out victory from defeat. At halftime, when the team's losing, what's the most important thing a coach can tell the team?"

"We can still win!" Gus answered.

"That's right! And the coach must give the team a picture of the win. The coach has to show the team members a picture of themselves on the medal stand, or holding up the trophy in triumph. They need to taste it, touch it, see it—they need a tangible reason to believe they can win! And you know where most of that's gotta come from? Deep inside the players!

"Don't hold this against me, but I've started studying words and where they come from. The word *encouragement* comes from the French *en coeur*. It means to be 'in heart.' When a person is encouraged, he's inspired with courage, spirit, and hope. The reason we lose our heart, lose our courage, is typically because we've lost hope. We lose confidence there's something good on the horizon. We've lost the belief that things can be different.

"It's one thing to get all motivated and fired up for one event or season. But the reason most motivational speakers, or gurus for that matter, don't do much to help a person change is because they don't teach the secret of how to replace discouragement with encouragement…it's not a once and done. It's daily. Like a leaky bucket, most of our inspiration or motivation doesn't last long. Motivational speakers pump us up, but that quickly dissipates. What we need is more inspiration. More vision of a hopeful purpose worth pursuing."

"Frankly, I cringe when I hear a lot of this motivational stuff," said Gus. "You can do it! Just try harder!"

"The best educated people in the world are not able to do much if they don't know how to get their hearts back when they lose them.

Most never learn that stuff. Sure, they may be able to name the state capitals and do trigonometry. But knowing how to get hope back when you've lost it?

"Hope changes things. Hope changes *everything*!

"And yet who's ever heard of a seminar or training on how to build more hope?

"Martin Luther said, *'Everything that is done in the world is done by hope.'* No hope, no lightbulbs. No hope, no airplanes. No hope, no cure for polio. No hope, no investments in anything with even the slightest bit of risk. Hope changes the neural pathways in the brain to make you enjoy the journey, not just the destination.

"And the Habits of Hope unlock all that intentionally, not just hit or miss! When you understand and encounter Hope, you're free to experience *now* in a powerful way. And you'll act now instead of dreading that it's not gonna matter or change much.

"I hope you don't mind me getting all preachy on ya, Gus, but I want to shout this message to the world. But most aren't listening! Yet! In fact, *yet* is a key hope word, isn't it? My marriage isn't great—*yet*! This company isn't growing—*yet*! This invention's not working—*yet*! I don't have a vision—*yet*!

"Hope's the key to creativity and to positive risk-taking. No successful entrepreneur ever succeeded without a large dose of hope. No academic achievement happens when you believe there's no hope of growing in knowledge or ability. No person on a spiritual quest arrives anywhere without hope."

Gus nodded in agreement as he pondered these words he knew were true.

"No one who climbs a mountain lacks hope. It's just not possible.

"No salesperson makes sales without hope.

"No parent overcomes the setbacks of parenting a tough child without hope.

"And no spouse remains married for a lifetime without hope. Hope changes everything!" Mr. Turnquest concluded.

"We need an extra dose of it in my and Amy's case!" Gus said. "Actually, I guess that's why I'm here!"

"Yeah, maybe so," said Mr. Turnquest. "The person who has hope has the will and determination that goals will be achieved and has a set of strategies to reach those goals. Put simply: hope involves the will to get there and different ways to get there. Hope's not just a feel-good emotion, but a dynamic process in the brain. Hope leads to learning goals, which are conducive to growth and improvement. Whether measured as a trait or a state, hope relates to positive outcomes.

"It's like athletes who win race after race. They possess hope they'll win. It's what keeps them practicing, sweating, and showing up at the starting line. My guess is that most athletes have higher levels of hope than non-athletes. We tend to define our reality by what we believe is possible."

"So why am I not able to change, Mr. T?" asked Gus. "I get this concept. I do."

"Just because something isn't happening for you right now doesn't mean it'll never happen. Hope's the little voice you hear whispering *maybe* when it seems the entire world is shouting *no*. Maybe I can. Maybe I can. Or the little engine that could. 'I think I can! I think I can!'"

"Mr. T, I love what you're saying. In here," Gus said, pointing to his head, "I think you're right. But there's a big gap here," he said, putting his hands on his heart.

"Yeah, it's that eighteen-inch gap that makes all the difference. If you asked someone, 'Do you want to be a person of hope?' my guess is he'd say, 'Of course!' We all like what we're like when hope lights us up!"

"So, will you walk the path to more hope? Hope as a way of life? That's the key."

"Why is that?" Gus asked.

"Well, most don't set out to be people of hope. And they don't know there's a way to get more of it. Kind of like getting more cash. But, Gus, that's where why I'm gonna share with you about the Habits of Hope and how they breed more hope—now and tomorrow. As long as you still believe history repeats itself, you'll stay stuck."

"Stuck. Yeah, I can relate to that word in particular," said Gus, nodding his head in agreement.

"A lot changes when your level of hope changes," said Mr. Turnquest. "Your health. Your relationships. Your ability to accomplish what you most want. Your financial situation. Sure, life's still got challenges and all, but hope helps you bounce back. However, if you don't believe things can change, you're right! They won't. You won't. So it takes some hope to head to hope. And the fact that you're here with me now says you've already begun. You're here now!

"Partner, I'm not saying hope's all rational. Sometimes, it doesn't make sense to believe. It's beyond the obvious and will require this thing called faith—believing what you can't see now or can't see yet."

"Yeah," said Gus. "My whole experience, my life, feels like it's stretching my faith pretty far."

"Gus, faith is complete trust and confidence in someone or something. It's 'Being sure of what you hope for, being convinced of what you can't see.' It's pretty easy to trust in what you can see. Now, what you can't see, including your future, your destiny, even your purpose being fulfilled—that's the stuff of faith. And so faith and hope are like brother and sister. They go together.

"Some think hopeful people are naive. They think you're a fool for believing. And even more, once you start practicing the Habits of Hope, people will wonder why you're wasting your time. And they've got a right to think that. But when you hope, your faith grows. When your faith grows, you hope more. When your hope muscle grows, you feel more equipped to imagine there's something worth hoping for.

"You'll start redefining what's probable or even possible, and doors you'd never dreamed of will open. The benefits of hope are like in that commercial for the credit card, 'priceless.' But there's a cost to pay to journey to hope. Are you interested in knowing the secret?"

"I'd be crazy not to want to know what you're talking about!" Gus replied.

CHAPTER 14

HABITS TO UNLOCK HOPE

"All our life, so far as it has definite form, is but a mass of habits."

— William James.

s the two men walked over to the side of the road and into a stand of trees, Mr. Turnquest pointed to a small evergreen sapling.

"Gus, would you do this? Go over and pull up that little sapling."

"Okay," said Gus, not quite sure where Turnquest was going with this.

After Gus had pulled the tree out of the ground, Mr. Turnquest said, "Now pull that one," and he pointed to one a few feet tall.

Gus chuckled, but then he did as his mentor instructed. He pulled it, but this time, it took a bit more pull and some leverage with his legs.

"Are we gonna start destroying the Adirondacks?"

"Hope not. But go pull that one," said Mr. Turnquest, pointing to a huge forty-foot tree.

"Not gonna happen. Unless we pull a crane in here or something!"

"Why is that?" Mr. Turnquest asked.

"Because that one's been around a while. It's got roots. It's attached."

"That, right there," said Mr. Turnquest, "is the power of developing a Habit of Hope, my friend. Life habits become the most powerful mechanisms for changing people's lives. Of course, we'd all love a magic pill! Just take this and you'll love life and be a success! But the way things work, you can't reap what you don't sow. And when you know what you want to grow, then you'll know the seed to plant.

"It says in the Bible, 'A man reaps what he sows.' And once you sow a new habit, it becomes your powerful way of life.

"People can change just like a planted seed can become a sapling. Start repeating an action, and over time it becomes part of you. Most of us don't realize how many habits we've accumulated since we were born.

"I've seen that in my own kids," said Gus. "Walk. Talk. Chew gum. Brush their teeth."

"And it's because they're habits, right? They're ingrained in them, and even when they're busy thinking about other things, they're automatic. It's almost as if they're compelled to do those things."

"I get it. Old habits are hard to break."

"Yeah. Good habits. Or bad habits. It's easier to pull up the sapling than the huge rooted tree. Habits tend to be the things that occur unconsciously. You're not thinking about them. Brain scientists would say they've been imprinted on our neural pathways. It's as if these little habit roads exist deep inside our brains."

Unconscious and Conscious Competence

"But aren't habits almost impossible to change for that very reason?" offered Gus.

"Yes. And no. Think about walking, Gus. We've been doing that all day. Walking is a good habit. At first, babies are not conscious of the habit—unconscious and incompetent. They can't walk, and they don't know it. But over time, babies notice they can't walk. Now they're conscious but still incompetent. 'Hey, all those big people do something I don't!'"

"Then babies ask for the car keys!" laughed Gus.

"Totally! But first those babies pull themselves up and start to walk, becoming toddlers. They become conscious and competent. They walk, but they have to think about it. It takes every ounce of baby concentration just to move one leg at a time. They're conscious-competent.

145

"Well, over time, these little people no longer think about how to walk when they walk. It becomes a habit. They're unconscious and competent."

"So unconscious competent—you don't think about it, but you do it all the time," said Gus, processing what Mr. Turnquest was saying.

"Yes. When you walk, Gus, you're not thinking about how to do it. You're moving your legs and shifting your weight. From the time you're a kid, you develop habits that become your way of life."

"Good ones and bad ones, right?" said Gus, showing his chewed fingernail.

"Yes! And frankly, Gus, some of those habits serve you. Some don't! Some build your life and make you freer and better. Others enslave you and you hardly know how you even became their prisoners!

"Most people don't start out saying, 'I'm gonna start doing things that make me unhealthy, angry, and isolated. I'm gonna become addicted. I'm gonna eat until I'm obese and get diabetes!' But we do things again and again, and they become our own hardwired traps— our little prisons of what we've learned to do!"

"I never imagined you as having many bad habits, Mr. T. Honestly, I kinda saw you as perfect!"

"Ha!" said Turnquest, with a burst of laughter. "That's a miss! Gus, I picked up a lot of bad habits along the way. My temper was one. I would tell people off. Shout at Alice and the kids as if I were barking.

"Clearly, I picked up that habit. Ask me how it's working for me?

"Smoking when I was in the army was another one for me. No sense of where it would lead or what it would do to my body. One day, someone handed me a lit cigarette and I took a puff. Then I bought a pack of my own. And before I knew it, I started smoking them when I was doing my work. It became hardwired in me. Work. Smoke. Have a beer. Smoke. Stressful day. Smoke. I didn't have any clue how hard it would be to kick that habit when I left the military. In some ways, it was as if smoking remade my brain and I hardly even noticed."

"How do you see changing those? Especially once they've become second nature to you?"

"Here's what I learned. I had to become conscious before I could change. 'Oh, my gosh! I'm smoking! And it's killing me little by little!

"Good habits act the same way. We reap what we sow. Sow good things, change everything, and remake the way you experience and do things. But you often need to replace the gunk that's clogging your brain and slowly stealing your life. Until I learned the Habits of Hope, I had plenty of habits. They just weren't life-giving habits. The Habits of Hope helped me make the changes I really wanted to make, but I was powerless to create.

"Bad habits tend to multiply other bad habits. I smoked. I combined smoking with drinking alcohol. Then I combined drinking alcohol with eating carbs—you know, chips, pretzels. Then that added to choosing not to exercise. You know the routine."

"All too well," agreed Gus.

"Habits of Hope create the pathways that open up the other doors.

They destroy fear and they empower you to live your dreams. When you lack the Habits of Hope, it's almost as if fear creeps into the crevices. You create a vacuum. Then you wonder why you're frustrated, or empty, or even depressed. You've basically let those habits of helplessness take over.

"Most people have no idea that's what they're doing! People without the Habits of Hope didn't set out to be unhappy, or discouraged, or depressed. They just didn't know what to do to get unstuck and make things better. And not just a bit better. Better on a whole other scale!" Mr. Turnquest said.

"How did this Habits of Hope thing start? Where did you find them? Who taught you them?" Gus asked.

"Ahh…now that's a great question!" Mr. Turnquest exclaimed.

"It's more of an obvious question at this point," Gus said. "You seem to talk about these things as if they were supernatural. Like coming from God or something. Did you make them up? Did you read about them somewhere?"

"Okay, so do you remember the letter you got from me inviting you to come to Hope?"

"How can I forget?"

"And do you remember the vision I had of you that I shared in the letter I put in the safety deposit box? What did I see you missing out on?" Mr. Turnquest asked.

"You saw me missing out on the bigger purpose of my life. You saw me missing out on meaning—a better story. In the future, you said you saw me affecting a God-sized change in the world. A *revolution* was the word you used!"

"Good memory!" affirmed Mr. Turnquest. "Gus, I'm crazy enough to believe that like me, you too were born for a bigger purpose. A destiny that was meant to be fulfilled. But the great enemy of the purpose-born is all that seeks to defeat that purpose. Most directly, the destruction of hope. So I'm here now to reactivate that hope. And when I reactivate that hope in you, guess what awaits?"

"What?" Gus asked, not quite sure.

"Your purpose! Your destiny! The very thing you were born to accomplish on planet earth!" Mr. Turnquest said. "No one gets to Hope on their own, Gus. People don't self-activate their real transformation. People empower others to become who they're supposed to be. Leaders build other leaders. Mentors create other mentors."

"Okay, I know you're wanting to bring this to me. But where did you come by these habits of hope?"

"When I was in the midst of my mess, I was living in Jersey, commuting every day to the city, to a job that sucked me dry. Alice was on the verge of leaving me. I received this letter from my wise friend, Henry. It was Henry who invited me to come to Hope."

"Are you serious?" said Gus, partly in disbelief.

"Totally serious! What I learned in that experience with Henry changed everything for me! I consider my life as BH and AH—Before Henry and After Henry! Or Before Hope and After Hope! And Henry taught me and became my coach, helping me to live the Habits of Hope."

"Where did Henry get them?"

"From what I remember, he also received them from someone in much the same way he passed them on to me. So all I can say is this way of life comes from God. Just the details are passed from person to person.

"I now realize that real change begins with one person changing, then helping another person change. When the person is ready, the teacher appears. It's God's way of showing up!

"Once I share the Habits of Hope with you, what you do with them will be up to you. But once you know, there's no going back. If you choose to stay the same and not put them into practice, it's almost worse than never knowing. *But...* the fact that you've already come this far and you're asking these questions means you're open. And being open says something."

"Well, if being open includes just about drowning, then I guess I'm open."

"Yep! Almost drowning may just be the best thing that ever happened. But you'll still need to choose. Are you ready to learn the first Habit of Hope?"

"Readier than ever!" Gus said. "And I mean that!"

"Awesome! I want to take you to see something. Hop in my Jeep. I'll drive."

CHAPTER 15

HEARING: HEARING "YOU'RE BLESSED!"

"Never forget who you are."

— *The Lion King*

As the two drove down Route 30 and headed out Route 8, Mr. Turnquest was quiet for a while. It was as if he were simply lost in the beauty of the mountains, with the windows open and sounds of the Jeep's well-tuned V-8 purring.

Finally, after about twenty minutes on Route 8, Turnquest broke the pleasant silence.

"Are you ready for the first Habit of Hope?"

"Ready," said Gus.

"The first Habit involves defeating the voice that wants to ruin every good thing. Each of us needs to hear, then dismiss that voice."

"And that 'voice' says what?"

"It says, 'You're cursed.' It's the 'You're no good' voice. It's that little voice that whispers in your inner ear: 'You're a no one. No one loves you. You're a loser.' Or even more medical terms that can end up defining us as being depressed, down, or discouraged. It's what the concept of 'waking up on the wrong side of the bed' means.

"At some time in life, almost all of us have been rejected, ignored, or wounded by words. We've experienced neglect or outright disgust. Someone out there was threatened by us, used us, and that lives on inside us. And it affects our vey identity. Who we are. It's the big lie. You're a nobody. You don't matter.

"God gets this."

"What do you mean, 'God gets this'?" Gus asked.

"Well, do you want to know the very first word spoken from heaven to Jesus? At least as recorded in the Bible?"

"Yes. What was it?" Gus asked.

"Even before Jesus himself started his public ministry at age thirty, God spoke from heaven in an audible voice and said, 'You are my beloved son, in whom I am well pleased.' That's right. Imagine that? If Jesus himself needed to hear from God that he was blessed and loved, don't you think we need that?"

"Totally!" said Gus. "Let's face it. Most of our earthly fathers didn't do too well with this one."

"And most boys, girls too, grow up without hearing who they are or that they're loved. Something's broken there! It's not our fault. Yet we all need to hear it from our earthly fathers, and few of us ever do. We all need someone whom we respect and believe in to tell us we're loved. And it should be someone who can speak to the very core of who we really are...whether we do anything recognized as great or not."

"Why is hearing we're blessed so connected to hope?" asked Gus.

"Hope will always be an *out there* thing unless you hear you're blessed—you're loved—and you take it in! You'll always be trying to earn being okay. You'll always feel a need to prove you're worthy...until you hear those words. And you'll fall short. *You've got to* believe those words, Partner. You've got to believe them as the key to your own identity, or you'll always be trying to fill an unfillable void."

"Do you believe you're blessed, Gus?" Mr. Turnquest asked.

"Ha!" Gus exclaimed. "Not really! I've had too much crap go wrong for me. Too much in my life that's not fit for a Hallmark card. My wife hates me. My kids don't respect me. I can't stand my job. I'm struggling to pay off my bills and not go deeper into debt. Shoot! Blessed? No."

"How would that change, Gus? How would you go from cursed to blessed?"

"Wish I knew," Gus mumbled.

Suddenly, without notice, Mr. Turnquest pulled the Jeep over on the dirt shoulder of the road.

"Where are we?" Gus asked.

"You've been here before," said Mr. Turnquest. "I want you to try to remember. Just close your eyes. Do you remember this place?"

Gus closed his eyes. He stood still for a second and then almost magically started to feel a cold wind hitting his face. A strange darkness enveloped him…something very unusual—like he'd never felt before.

"Can you see it, Gus?"

Gus was blinded by glaring red emergency lights and headlights. He was standing on the side of this same dark road lit by the red lights. Snow was falling, and he was standing up to his ankles in it.

"What in the world?" Gus exclaimed, shocked by the sudden change. "I remember! I have been here before!" Gus said, seeing this sight as if in a vivid dream.

"You're right, Gus," said Mr. Turnquest. "You've been here before. Do you recognize that really upset man in the red ski jacket standing next to the car?"

"No, I don't think so. Wait. Oh, my God! That's my father! My father? But he looks really young!" Gus said.

"That's right. He's actually the age you are now. And he's just experienced one of the most traumatizing events of his life. A car coming over that hill lost control and careened head on into him. His beloved son was in the front seat," Mr. Turnquest said. "Do you remember that car?"

"Yes! Well. No! I went face first into the dashboard. I lost consciousness. I blacked out. I was just ten years old."

"You see that little boy crying in the front seat of that mangled car? Does he look familiar?"

"Oh, my God! Yeah, that's me! That's me!" Gus exclaimed.

"Your father came close to losing everything that really mattered to him that snowy night on Route 8. Look at how your car barely balanced on the precipice of the road. Another inch or two to the right, and you, your dad, your brother, and your friends in that car would have been crushed by the fall. How do you feel seeing ten-year-old you?"

"Blown away! Bizarre! And I feel for him! He's in shock. He's clearly out of it. His nose, face, mouth are full of blood," Gus said. "Why am I seeing this, Mr. T?"

"Because someone wanted you dead that night. The enemy of your life wanted you dead. The same enemy that sought to abort you before you were born. Gone. But your life has been spared on purpose. Your life and the lives of everyone in that car."

"Why?"

"Because there's a bigger plan for you and that's why you're still here! You're not only *not* cursed, you're blessed. Called. Chosen. On Purpose. You're a son. Do you remember what happened when your own father saw you?"

157

"No. Not really. Should I?"

"Your father wept! He wrapped you in his arms. Even though he too was bruised from the accident, he treasured his son. 'Oh, Gus. Oh, Gus,' he cried as he held you. Tears fell freely from his eyes and drenched your shirt. 'Are you okay? Gus. Gus! I'm so sorry! I'm so sorry!'"

As Gus began to recall, tears began to roll down his own face. "I hadn't remembered ever seeing my father cry. At least, I didn't know I had," said Gus.

"Gus, for some reason it was blocked from your memory. But you do know it happened. And you know you weren't killed that night. And now you know just how much your own father was grateful you were alive. He loved you.

"And even more importantly, your life matters to God. You didn't die in that accident. That was no accident! You're a child of God. From the time you were born, you were meant to be an over-comer. Actually, more than an over-comer. You're more than a conqueror! That's exactly what Paul said in the book of Romans. 'If God is for you, who can be against you?' And you are more than a conqueror. Not only a conqueror. You're more than a conqueror! More than!"

"How do you see this as a Habit?"

"HEARING you're blessed is intentionally rejecting the voice that wants you dead, defeated, and discouraged, and intentionally tuning in to the other voice: 'More than a conqueror. Blessed. Not cursed! Blessed!' Hope's got the right foundation!

"The first Habit of Hope is just that: HEARING. Hearing you're blessed. Hearing your real identity.

"Every other Habit of Hope depends on it. It's the *why* behind everything. God not only created you to exist; you're created to be a conqueror. Actually more than a conqueror!

"Too many hear rogue voices telling them, 'You're a nobody! You're no one special. Your life doesn't matter!'

The Jewish writer Abraham Heschel said, "The greatest sin of man is to forget he's a prince."

"Do you know what the other voice people hear is, Gus?"

"What?"

"'Prove yourself. Prove you've got value! You're not wanted!' That's why so many struggle to have hope! That's just not the case!" Mr. Turnquest said, his face turning red with passion.

"You're blessed. Your identity's one of royalty. You're a child of your dad and a child of God. You're the son of a king! You matter! You're here for a reason!"

"I can see you're pretty passionate about this. I've never seen you so wound up," Gus said.

"Gus, this identity lie is a disease! It's killing great people. Great kids, too! When so many voices aim to take down our identity, you've got to hear the other voice! The voice of God! As soon as you wake up and see daylight, or even turn on the light, hear, 'You are blessed.

159

"You're not cursed! Do you hear me? No matter how you've failed or what you've done, you're a child! More than a conqueror! *Hear* you are blessed. Don't prove anything. Listen to hear God say that to you, 'I bless you.'"

"How does that become a habit for you?" asked Gus.

"Create a reminder near your bed or near the coffeepot, if that helps. 'You're blessed!' The first thought you can look forward to each day when your eyes open can be, 'Wow! A new day! I'm blessed!'

"Gus, this habit changes everything! Everything! When you hear you're blessed, you can't help but start ignoring the other voices thrown at you all day: Be afraid? Nope, blessed. Worry? Not today! Blessed! Be anxious? Fearful? Not a chance! Knowing your true identity robs fear of its power over you. It breaks those nasty chains! It kills fear.

Fear Not!

"Do you realize that *fear not*—or words to that effect—is the most repeated command in the Bible. Some calculate it at 365 times! One for each day of the year! The voice of fear will do all it can to keep you from hearing 'You're blessed.'

"Gus, you're not alone in this struggle. Every human being has to battle against being falsely labeled or accused by the voice of fear. Fear says, 'You're an orphan. You're cursed. You're life's not precious. You don't matter.'

"However, the 'HEARING You're Blessed' habit defeats that voice.

And there's no better time to win that war than as soon as you open your eyes and see the light each morning. See the light. Hear you're blessed! Say the words out loud until you can't not think them. As you see the light of each new day, just say, 'I'm blessed!' I know most people don't do that! I know it may seem awkward. But when you realize each day is a gift you've been given, you won't take it for granted.

"You can't bless others until you realize you're blessed. Why? Because you'll be needing something from them that they can't give you. You'll need their approval. Without hearing you're blessed, you'll look to your status to define you—how much money you have, etc.

"You matter! Your life has value. You're here for a purpose! You may not yet see it, and you haven't seen it in the past. But today is a new day for you. In fact, you may want to repeat those words out loud.

"I am loved. I am blessed. I am courageous.

"Let that identity seep deeply into your soul. Open yourself to the love as one who God shows favor on, and let that become who you are at the very core of your being. Whenever you hear a whisper that says, 'You're a no one. Not important!' Counter with, and hear, 'You're blessed.'

"Let this become the foundation of your confidence and your purpose, as one who's very life wasn't an accident. No! You're a chosen one! A child of God! Blessed! Blessed! Blessed!"

Habit of Hope:

Hearing "You're Blessed!"

Summarized: Defeat the voices of fear and cursing that want to ruin every good thing. Intentionally tune in to the truth of your real identity as one who is loved, blessed, and courageous.

Realized: What benefit or benefits might you (and/or others) see or experience by you practicing this habit of *Hearing "You're Blessed!"* as a way of life?

Evaluated: How far along are you in this habit of *Hearing "You're Blessed!"* presently? (1 not at all to 10 completely)

    1   2   3   4   5   6   7   8   9   10

Applied: What will you do to practice or grow the habit of *Hearing "You're Blessed!"*?

Habit Releaser:

Read the Bible or other positive and encouraging books that speak truth and courage at the start of each day.

Listen to music that speaks powerful truth, positive affirmations, or worship of God. (For example: "No Longer a Slave to Fear" by Bethel Music)

Practice quieting yourself each day and noticing the words in your mind. Don't force them to change, but just tune in to them. As you become aware of them, note whether they are thoughts of blessing or thoughts of curses, fear, or lies. Gently dismiss the negative voices.

CHAPTER 16

APPRECIATING: APPRECIATING THE GOOD

"Hope makes you see God's guiding hand not only
in the gentle and pleasant moments but also in the
shadows of disappointment and darkness."

— Henri Nouwen

s the two drove back toward Hope, Gus was already
starting to feel just a tinge more hope.

Then a question popped into Gus' mind.

"Honestly, Mr. T, I feel great right now. My challenge is I'm so
inconsistent. I have one good day, then a bad one. Actually, let me
correct that. One good hour, then a lousy one. Then I get into a
sink hole of anger and disappointment and begin to spiral down."

"Okay," Mr. Turnquest said, "then you're ready for Habit of Hope number two: *Appreciating*. Appreciating the good.

"This habit relates to the first one, but it's getting more specifically into all the little ways you really are blessed. Gus, I spent a long time, decades even, trying to balance out all the things that were wrong with the things that were supposedly right. And somehow, the wrong things seemed to take the day.

"Let me show you something. You see this piece of paper?" Mr. Turnquest picked up a white piece of copy paper. Then he took a black pen and drew a mark right in the center. He held it up in front of them.

"What do you see?"

"A black dot," Gus quickly responded, wondering whether Mr. Turnquest had some trick up his sleeve. Was it a trick question? "Why? What do you see?"

"A white piece of paper," said Turnquest, with a smile. "Oh, yeah, it's got a dot in the center. But 99.9 percent of it is a white piece of paper."

"Ha!" laughed Gus. "Okay. I can see your point!"

"The appreciating habit is about changing your whole mindset—what you see when you see. It's about changing your vision of what's going on all around you. Incredible things!

"You see, I used to think negative thinking wasn't that big a deal and didn't have much effect. 'Positive thinking' was just a soft and fluffy term that's easy to dismiss. Psycho junk. It didn't have much real world relevance.

"Gus, was I wrong about that! Very wrong!"

What Negative Thoughts Do to the Brain

"As we allow our thinking to become tuned to seeing negative and fearful thoughts as true, we develop patterns of thought that cloud our whole souls—it snowballs."

"What do you mean by 'snowballs?' Like it grows?" asked Gus.

"Grows and takes over the good thoughts! When threatened by imminent danger, our brains become hard-wired to shut down all other options. If you're walking in the jungle and a tiger jumps out, your neural connections don't consider many alternatives. They get the heck out of there!

"Your every thought releases brain chemicals. When you focus on negative thoughts, you sap the brain of its energy. That shuts down neural pathways and dims your brain's ability to function fully.

"Ever get in a fight with someone?"

"Uh, totally!" Gus said. "More with my wife than I'd care to talk about!"

"What controls you in the midst of that fight?"

"The anger, usually. Emotion! Logic would be nice. But that's often not the case."

"When you're in a fight with someone, just think of how the anger and emotion becomes your focus to the point where you can hardly think of anything else. Stress and negative thoughts make it hard to think about anything else, right? The black dot becomes all there is! Basically, you don't need to be a brain surgeon to understand how that slowly kills our brains, not to mention our souls!

"Jesus certainly taught this from a spiritual perspective. 'Therefore I tell you, do not worry about your life, what you will eat or drink; or about your body, what you will wear. Is not life more than food and the body more than clothes?' Jesus' words in the book of Matthew were peace-giving:

"'Look at the birds of the air; they do not sow or reap or store away in barns, and yet your heavenly Father feeds them. Are you not much more valuable than they? Can any one of you by worrying add a single hour to your life?'

"Soothing words, right? That's what we need more of. But negative thoughts tell God, tell the universe, and tell ourselves: 'All is not well! There's danger! Danger!' Our brains then go into lockdown mode!

Jesus taught: Change your focus. Instead of allowing the fearful and damaging thoughts to take hold, 'Seek first the kingdom of God and His righteousness. Then all these things shall be added to you.'

"Move from being 'what's really wrong focused' to 'what's really right focused,'" Mr. Turnquest concluded.

What Positive Thoughts Do to the Brain

"When you think positive, happy, hopeful thoughts, it's as if your brain breathes. It's like the oxygen it really needs for health. Such thoughts decrease cortisol and produce serotonin, which creates a sense of wellbeing. Your brain feels like it flows. Peaceful. Full.

"Keep your peace. Keep your heart. Keep your mind.

"Gus, it doesn't take much medical knowledge to diagnose that St. Paul was right on when he told us to think on 'Whatever is true, whatever is noble, and whatever is right.' Frankly, this works wonders!

"I've heard this. It's true for sure. But how do you put that into practice?" asked Gus.

"Practice this habit of appreciating at the start of and throughout the day. Say what's good out loud. Write it down. Then watch as your appreciation stimulates the growth of nerve connections, improves your thinking, deepens your ability to think things through, and affects the lens through which you see everything around you!

"Other than making us much more fun to be around, being happy opens us up to see more hope all around us! Basically, when you learn how to see the good *and* appreciate the good, it makes your whole life become a miracle!" Mr. Turnquest said.

Here's the Simple Habit: Write Out Your Appreciation of What Is

Mr. Turnquest went on, "As soon as you wake up each morning, write what you're grateful for and what you appreciate. At the beginning of each day, redirect your mind to what is good, what is pure, and what is true.

"Everyone in Hope starts the day in appreciation. It's our version of a morning siesta! We make a list of all we can think of to appreciate. We write it in a list. I simply sit down in my favorite place and note what I'm grateful for.

"Recognize that each of the things on your list are the gifts of God. They're given to you for your enjoyment and your pleasure. It's almost how you end up seeing who God really is at the start of every day, and it leaks all over you.

"Do it on a piece of paper. Start a gratitude journal. Put it in your smart phone. Do it on your computer. Do it whatever way works for you.

"It doesn't need to take long. Just write the date. Then start listing what you can think of to appreciate.

"Here's what I wrote on my list yesterday:

- Gorgeous morning in the mountains
- Feeling great this morning physically
- Great dinner last night with steak and corn on the cob
- Fun exercise time with Frank on the bike
- Plan to hike today
- How powerfully I feel the love for my sons
- The toilet works again!
- Love my dogs!
- Time to be with Gus

"You see, nothing all that interesting. The key: noticing.

"Notice all the white paper! Notice all that God has given you as a gift. And Gus, there are too many days behind us when we might have missed the magic of the *now*! All the great things we've been given *now* are all right here in the moment.

"I never regret starting my day by listing my appreciation! Never ever! It's almost as if it bathes me in peace. It's like oil for this rusty brain. Refreshing every time. And the cost? Maybe just the paper. Or some people may do it on their computer or whatever. Just as long as it's a place you can keep doing it the next day.

"That's really good," said Gus. It's simple too. Doable."

"Very doable! And as you create appreciating as a habit, it's as if the neurons in your brain rewire to see, experience, and even find more that's good all around you. You can change your brain. You just need to do it intentionally.

"Start appreciating today! You don't need to wait," Mr. Turnquest said.

Habit of Hope:
Appreciating the Good

Summarized: Intentionally change your focus from fearful and damaging thoughts by replacing those with all that is good. Change your brain! Find things in your life and surroundings to be grateful for and actively note them in lists of appreciation.

Realized: What benefit or benefits might you (and/or others) see or experience by you practicing the habit of *Appreciating the Good* as a way of life?

Evaluated: How far along are you in the habit of *Appreciating the Good* presently? (1 not at all to 10 completely)

    1   2   3   4   5   6   7   8   9   10

Applied: What will you do to practice or grow the habit of *Appreciating the Good*?

Habit Releaser:

Create your appreciation list in a place that works for you. You may use a journal, an app on a smartphone, or a file on your computer.

For the next thirty days, start your day by sitting quietly before breakfast and just listing things you appreciate. Even if it's simple ("It's sunny today" or "money to buy food"), write what comes to mind.

Note how your body and mind feel after you practice this.

Extra: Write your appreciation before you go to sleep at night.

CHAPTER 17

BELIEVING: BELIEVING GOD IS AT WORK AND JOINING HIM

"We don't choose what we will do for God; He invites us to join Him where He wants to involve us."

— Henry T. Blackaby

After they enjoyed a good, hardy, but healthy lunch of fresh salad and the "Chicken Aspen" up at the Melody Lodge restaurant, with a view that looked more like a painting than real life, Turnquest invited Gus into the next adventure of Hope.

"I want to take you somewhere else you've been before," said Mr. Turnquest. "But my guess is you haven't seen it quite this way."

They walked over to Mr. Turnquest's Jeep Grand Cherokee, and this time, Turnquest asked Gus to drive.

As they drove north on Route 30, the magic of the mountain views overwhelmed them. The windows were wide open as the unseasonably warm air filled the car. They passed lakes on either side of the road and went down and up as if on a roller coaster.

"Gus," said Mr. Turnquest, looking over, "the biggest spiritual lie floated around these days is that God no longer works in the world. It's almost as if God is limited to ancient times or religious services."

"Yeah," said Gus, "I'll admit I'm uncomfortable with a lot of organized religion or spirituality that tries to have all the answers about God…what God can and can't do. But I'm curious about how I might access a deeper connection with God in the here and now. I pray. I believe in God."

"Gus, It's possible not to be an atheist but act like one. Most of us do that. Sure, we say we believe in God, but when it comes right down to it, trust isn't much a part of our lives. I can say a creed or whatever, but it's another thing to believe God is at work in the world today. And not just *the* world, but *my* world—*your* world," Mr. Turnquest said with a clear emphasis on the word *your*.

"Okay. You have my attention," said Gus. "How does one see God at work in the world? And do it as a habit?"

"God wants to create something awesome through you and me. Actually, He wants us to join us in the work He's already doing in the world."

"What do you mean by the 'work God's already doing in the world?"

"Well, God's not done creating a better world. Clearly the perfect world God created has been tarnished and polluted. That's the story of the first few chapters of Genesis. Call it the fall. Sin. Very much not the way things were meant to be. But God hates the injustice, poverty, sickness, and decay more than we do. And He invites us to the greatest adventure of all time. The adventure of restoring what's broken and bad in people and in the world.

God wants us to be a part of a bigger work. And God's got a much bigger destiny than we can ever imagine for us...*if*—*if* we'll let God do it. God invites us—but won't force us.

"Jesus said He came to build a Kingdom. 'The Kingdom of God is near you. It's like a mustard seed. It seems faint at first, but grows into something awesome.' Not a someday when you get to heaven Kingdom. A here and now thing! Changing the world by bringing more of heaven to earth.

"The biggest thing happening in the world right now, Gus— though hardly ever reported by the media—is God is building the Kingdom. God is creating powerful transformation to a better way of life on planet earth for people and for creation. God's moving us from scarcity to abundance, from hatred to love, from greed to generosity. All that stuff we worry so much about, Gus—enough money, food, housing. God said, 'Seek first the Kingdom of God... and all this will be added on to you.'"

Gus just listened and nodded, trying to take in words that on one level made it feel like Mr. Turnquest was speaking a foreign tongue. Yet on another level, it was as if his whole life had been in preparation to hear just this—believing God is at work...and joining him!

"The God who created you wants to create something with you and through you each day! God building the kingdom is God establishing a culture of people on earth who aren't all worried about get-get-get.... They're not caught up in getting by until they can one day retire and live comfortably. No! They're experiencing the very purpose they were created for. They're flourishing and helping build human flourishing in every single person in the world.

"The greatest tragedy isn't when people die young. It's when they live their whole lives without ever knowing or experiencing their purposes," said Turnquest, with fiery passion in his eyes.

The two exited Route 30 and made their way through some winding roads that eventually turned to dirt before they came to a small Boy Scouts camp.

They parked, then walked across a field of grass to a sign reading "The Chimney Mountain Trailhead."

They hiked the rocky trail, talking as they walked, until they arrived at the summit. At the summit, they came to a rocky structure jutting out of the edge of a steep cliff, which overlooked miles and miles of Adirondack beauty. It was a spire of rocks looming high.

The hike was shorter than Gus remembered, and as he hiked, the words he had just heard bounced around his head. "The great tragedy isn't death. It's to live never knowing one's purpose." Why was Mr. Turnquest the only one who seemed to talk like this?

"Recognize this place, Gus?" Turnquest asked, bringing Gus back to the here and now.

"I've always loved Chimney Mountain!" Gus exclaimed, in an almost childlike voice. "Sure, I know this place! I love this place! I climbed up here many times over the years."

"Why, Gus? Why this place? Why do you climb up here?"

"Frankly, because from up here it seems like I can see the whole Adirondacks. You get basically a 360-degree view, and you feel like you're on top of the world. Seemingly endless peaks in every direction."

"Gus, the first time I climbed up here, I hiked up with my own father and brother. The trail wasn't quite what it is today, so we had to bushwhack part of the way. But when I saw this view, especially after climbing around this side of the Chimney…my father asked me a question. I remember it like it was yesterday. He asked, 'What do you see?' In typical teenage fashion, I said, 'Mountains. Sky. Clouds. Why, Dad?'

"'Rodney,' he said, 'I see God at work all around. When I see these mountains, I see that God is incredibly creative. And that same God who created these mountains is still creating things in this here world of ours.'"

As the two stared off over the mountains, the reds, yellows, and greens jutted out, creating a magic canvas of color. They could see the top of Snowy Mountain….

"Go back to the beginning of the Bible, Gus. What's God doing?"

"He's creating the world. 'In the beginning, God created the heavens and the earth.'"

"Bull's-eye! And what's God doing these days?"

"I'm not always so sure. In actuality, I hunger to be part of what God does. I really just don't know how to gauge it. And, honestly, I've been pretty distracted."

"God's still creating! God's building the Kingdom of Hope in a world that's been darkened. God's about the work of creating human flourishing in the world. God's creating real wealth...the wealth of human beings who get to experience real richness in every part of their lives.

"This same God who created these mountains still creates! God's at work orchestrating something better than what exists. God's not any different from the God who created the heavens and the earth. God wants to be in relationship with you...and has invited you to join in the greatest adventure of all time! Literally!

"Would you mind if I share a brief history of the universe with you, Gus? I mean, it's really the context for all that happens in Hope."

"Go for it!" Gus said, not sure what he was getting himself into.

God's Great Desire

"Okay, so God creates the universe and displays creative genius—from creating giant light and energy-producing bodies to DNA that replicates living beings—from whales to walruses. But God's greatest desire...do you know what it is?"

"What?" Gus asked.

"It's connecting with you and having you join in building His world of humans flourishing in the world. The Jews called it Shalom. Peace. In Genesis 1, everything was Shalom. Wellbeing was all over the earth.

God invites you join Him in restoring that wellbeing! That peace. That Shalom. As a human being, you're part of creation...but also as different from every other thing God created: God made man and woman in God's own image to do something special. 'Rule over creation. Make something great with God.'

"You can read right in Genesis 1:26, *"Let us make mankind in our image, in our likeness, so that they may rule over the fish in the sea and the birds in the sky, over the livestock and all the wild animals, and over all the creatures that move along the ground."* Human beings should 'rule,' or in the Hebrew, 'radah,' which translates as 'reign' or 'build kingdom.'

"The overarching theme of the Bible is not to 'get people saved,' 'populate heaven,' or make people 'more religious.' It's about God wanting to connect with people in a real relationship to 'Love God.'" Then God invites us to do things that transform the world and create love everywhere else. 'Love your neighbor.'

"And that includes every inch of the planet. From hedge funds on Wall Street to better health care, hospitals, and healing between races. It's clean water in Africa. Better jobs in cities. It's companies where people feel empowered to contribute and build community instead of feeling like cogs in a wheel. 'Your Kingdom come, your will be done on earth as it is in heaven.'

"Do you see yourself building a flourishing kingdom as the main purpose you exist?"

"Not really," said Gus. "But I wish I did. And I don't think I'm alone. Why don't most people live this way?"

"Now, you know that the rest of the Bible contains the story of human rebellion against God, about the first humans, our forefathers, rejecting God and all that entailed. Then it's the story of all God does to restore the relationship and a way of life that was lost. The Bible begins with God's creation of flourishing and shalom. Hope. But the story we've all walked in to is one of hope lost."

"And you see that as that big deal?"

"That's a big deal! A huge deal! God wants to restore hope and restore authentic relationship *and* restore you and all people as co-leaders of the earth with God.

"And we've forgotten God wants us to join the King in creating good things. Solving problems. Establishing a way of abundant life, not just survival. Jesus called it a Kingdom. And God rules that Kingdom. But unlike most earthly kingdoms, God doesn't seek to create loyal subjects. God's not out to subdue and dominate. No! God calls us royal heirs. Children. And God desperately wants us not just to survive, but to flourish and help bring God's kind of flourishing to every part of creation."

"That sounds incredible!" said Gus, with more enthusiasm than he'd shown in a long time. "So, you think that's pretty important, huh?"

"Once again. Big yes! Despite the blindness to it, there's absolutely nothing more important happening on the earth today. It involves the retaking of territory that's been trapped in darkness. God is colonizing the earth…but not to dominate it. Instead to restore it. To recreate it."

"And the 'Believing God's at work and joining in that work' habit?"

"That's your individual access. It has everything to do with why hope is *so* acutely absent from most human beings today. Most have no idea God is doing something significant in the world, *and* they have no idea God's inviting them in to be co-creators in it. When you join the bigger story of creating flourishing in the world, and get to be part of it, you can't miss experiencing the bigger purpose of your life as a side-benefit."

Your Involvement in the Bigger Plan

"Mr. T, you seem convinced God has a plan for us," said Gus. "What would that look like in a world that's still so messed up?"

"It's certainly different for different people. But, involvement in God's work creates in you a deep hope for the work you do day to day. A clarity and a confidence. A purpose, not just a paycheck. Creating value instead of extracting value. You'd know that you're on a mission to push back darkness, bring order from chaos, and solve problems on earth. You would never retire from being involved in God's work and seeing God's Kingdom come. You wouldn't want to!"

"Your kingdom come, huh? I wondered what that meant," said Gus.

"'Kingdom come' is God's desire to bring the creativity, culture, and way of life of heaven back to earth. It's God's Kingdom colonizing earth and creating deeper community, more harmony, economic justice, and prosperity. Again, human flourishing. Shalom on earth. Peace. It's the best government ever! Jesus said His main goal was to preach the good news of the Kingdom. It's good news!"

Practicing BELIEVING God Is at Work

"So how do you know when you're practicing the habit of BELIEVING God's at work and joining in Mr. T?"

"Jesus was pretty clear. 'But seek first the kingdom of God and his righteousness.' One first priority. Just one! 'What shall I do today?' 'Seek first God's Kingdom.' Then, and only then, 'would all these things be given to you as well.' God really does want you to have all you need to fulfill your bigger purpose in the world. However, that's what's added as a side benefit. Not the main deal! Health and wealth aren't the reason you're here.

"BELIEVING God's at work and joining in certainly would mean you're not wasting any time worrying about things that kill hope day to day. How to pay bills. How to clothe yourself. 'What you will eat or drink or what you will wear.' Whenever you're worried, fearful, or frustrated, the light on your dashboard should go on.... 'Warning: Not BELIEVING God is at work.'"

"Yeah, I think that light must be on a lot for me lately," offered Gus.

"I would imagine," agreed Mr. Turnquest. "But that stops now! You don't have to be enslaved. Really!

"Back to your question…. You also know you're practicing the BELIEVING habit when you consciously look around and notice places God is at work. Where in your world is God wanting to bring about freedom, opportunity, or love? Where is God wanting to bring order to something that's a mess? Who's being abused and in need of justice? Who needs support and help not just to survive, but to flourish? Who's struggling to get by and needs a good job?"

"What about when you're more bummed out and bugged by things than noticing who needs your help?"

"Take note of what bugs you! When something bugs you, and you feel like things need to change, that can be a key to knowing the work God wants you to do. That's right. You! What do you see that needs to change? Could it be that it just so happened that you were especially equipped, gifted—and you care enough—to do something God wants done?

"Until you start to actively believe that God is at work around you and seek that, you will always be disappointed with what you have and need. But God wants to connect your desire for a bigger purpose with His bigger purpose.

"Part of God's Kingdom mission. 'Seek first his Kingdom and his righteousness' was the path Jesus promised would lead to God, 'adding everything else.'"

"Sounds like you believe God's Kingdom is really good news, even today. Maybe even the Hope of the world!" said Gus.

"With all my heart! It's not doing stuff as an end in itself. God didn't create religion made of human rules and regulations. His work isn't to create vacant institutions filled with power and control. When love's not there, God's not at work. Even good things like education when they become an end in and of themselves spoil things. Being smart without a purpose or a vision for your education can feel meaningless. Instead, God's work is an adventure of Kingdom building in the world! Now that's where hope comes from and where hope grows exponentially!"

Believe God Is at Work *Today*…and Ask God, "Where Can I Join You?"

"Are there any key questions you ask yourself or God to know what to do?" asked Gus.

"Literally, ask God, 'Where are You working today God?' Then just listen.

"You may want to keep a pen and paper near you. Sometimes, I write down what I hear."

"What kinds of things do you hear?" Gus asked.

"When I listen," Mr. Turnquest replied, "sometimes I hear things like, 'I am working *in* you. I'm developing your trust. I'm teaching you how to be happy.' But I've also heard things like, 'In kids who need encouragement and to see their "Why."' 'In helping business owners get funding to create more jobs.' 'In a single dad needing better childcare….' 'In women who are being called to higher levels of leadership and freedom in business and organizations.'

"God is at work all around us. It's our job to see it. To experience it. To join the opportunity. Remember this great view! Every time you see a beautiful vista, Gus, remember: The God who created this incredible view is at work creating more beautiful things in the world.

"Every time you're not in the Adirondacks but you're captivated by a sunrise, a forest, a blue sky, or even a thunderstorm, remember that the God who created that is at work in the world and making it great. Then ask: 'Where can I join you?'"

Habit of Hope:

Believing God Is at Work and Joining Him

Summarized: Practice looking for places and ways God is at work building His Kingdom all around you in the world. See yourself as involved in God's bigger purpose and let that create in you deep enjoyment and significance for the work you do every day.

Realized: What benefit or benefits might you (and/or others) see or experience by you practicing the habit of *Believing God Is at Work and Joining Him* as a way of life?

Evaluated: How far along are you in the habit of *Believing God Is at Work and Joining Him* presently? (1 not at all to 10 completely)

    1   2   3   4   5   6   7   8   9   10

Applied: What will you do to practice or grow the habit of *Believing God Is at Work and Joining Him*?

Habit Releaser:

Practice saying this prayer as you begin your day or approach some challenge: "Your Kingdom come, your will be done, on earth as it is in heaven."

In a journal or in your prayer as you start your day, write or say the words, "Where are you at work, God?" Then listen and note what your hear.

Take action to follow through tangibly in the place you sense God is at work and is inviting you to join Him.

CHAPTER 18

INVESTING: INVESTING IN YOURSELF AND YOUR DREAMS

"Each day is filled with thousands of opportunities to change the stories of our lives."

— Michael Hyatt

G us and Mr. Turnquest hiked back down Chimney Mountain and drove back to Hope, taking the scenic road around the lake.

"I want you to see something," Mr. Turnquest said, pulling over in front of a driveway along South Shore Road.

They got out of the car and walked down a long driveway toward the lake to a great looking classic Adirondack cottage right on Lake

Hope. The yellow leaves lined the driveway, and the sun peeked through them.

Then Mr. Turnquest clasped the bottom of a garage door and hoisted it. Behind the door were two classic automobiles.

"See that?" asked Mr. Turnquest, pointing to one of the vehicles. "It's a mint condition World War II Willys CJ 2A, but most people just call it a jeep. It was restored by the Bundy family and now rides in the Fourth of July parade in town each year."

"Wow! Love that!" Gus said. "I know nothing about classic cars like that. But I know quality when I see it!"

"And check this out," said Mr. Turnquest. "Do you know what this is?"

"A beautiful old pickup truck?"

"It's a 1940 Ford, restored to mint condition by Ed Holly. He's made sure I know it has a 239 Ford Flathead V8, with a three-speed transmission. One of the great trucks of the day."

"Wow! Not a scratch on that thing!" Gus exclaimed, gently running his hand over the perfectly smooth red paint.

"Okay, are you ready for a short field trip?"

"This whole experience has been a field trip! Sure."

"I'm going to take you on a little walk. But hop in the car; it's actually down at the other end of the lake."

Gus and Mr. Turnquest once again hopped into Mr. Turnquest's car and drove around the other side of Lake Pleasant. As they did, the cool breeze flooded in the window. They had to slow down as three deer walked across the road, almost acting as if they saw the car as just a slight annoyance.

The men drove up a dirt road at the other end of the lake and parked where it ended and became a path. Over the next fifteen minutes, they walked together down a trail filled with all the sounds of fall in the Adirondacks.

As they walked, Mr. Turnquest noted the sounds of a Swainson's thrush, followed by a white-throated sparrow, a winter wren, and a rose-breasted grosbeak.

"Shh," said Mr. Turnquest stopping in his tracks. "That's an olive-sided flycatcher! Do you hear that pit-pit-pit sound?"

They walked a little farther, and again, Mr. Turnquest stopped in his tracks.

"That's a black and white throated sparrow. Listen. Doesn't it sound like it's singing O, sweet Canada-Canada-Canada?"

"Well, I guess so, now that you mention it! That's pretty cool!" Gus said.

"Okay, now look to your right. Do you see that?" said Turnquest, pointing to something on the right of the path.

"Wow! It sure seems like it's seen some better days. It's an old, rusted vehicle."

"Do you know what kind of vehicle that is, Gus?"

"Not quite sure. Maybe some kind of truck?"

"Yep. It's a truck. Actually, a 1940 Ford pickup."

"Same year and make as the one we just saw in the garage. Wow! Wow! Wow! What a difference! Oh, my God!"

"That's what I wanted you to see, Gus! One's been cared for, invested in, and doted upon. The other's been neglected, overlooked, and abandoned."

"Wow! Pretty amazing contrast!"

"Do you know what rust actually is, Gus?"

Answering before Gus could respond, Turnquest explained, "Given sufficient time, oxygen, and water, any iron object will eventually convert entirely to rust and disintegrate. It's natural. Without protection against the elements, iron things actually turn into something they weren't…rust.

"Over time, the oxygen combines with the metal at an atomic level, forming a new compound called an oxide. And it weakens the bonds of the metal itself. The metal ceases to function the way it was created to function. Iron and metal that just sit there are sitting ducks! They corrode and disintegrate. They need some kind of input or their identity and strength go away. And that's why you need to get this visual in your mind."

"So my guess is this must relate to another Habit of Hope, right?" asked Gus.

194

"Yep! Like that truck, those who don't continually invest in themselves will end up rusted on the outside, but also on the inside…the parts we can't see—the you in you. Your mind. Your strength. Your soul.

"INVESTING in yourself and in your dreams is a key habit for those wanting to live in Hope.

"It says in the Bible we are to love God with all our heart, soul, mind, and strength. Right?"

"Yeah," agreed Gus.

"Then what comes next?" asked Mr. Turnquest.

"And love our neighbor as we love ourselves," replied Gus.

"Do you realize it's really easy to miss a key part of that concept? Even unintentionally?"

"What?"

"It's the 'as you love yourself part.' You can't do much good in loving others, including your own spouse or family, if you don't know how to love yourself. And to love yourself, you've consciously got to invest in yourself.

"Do you know how I can recognize the sounds of those birds? I've taken classes on it. I've actually paid people to help me know bird sounds! But you know what, Gus? That investment added value to lives…mine and others! The reason many people lack hope is they don't love themselves enough to invest in their own growth. They don't make themselves the best them they can.

"Most people create a poverty mindset around the thing they can least afford to be poor toward. Themselves. I've watched it over and over. Give people something for free, and they think it's a trap. Tell them it's a small investment, they'll say they can't earn that much. Encourage them to try something different, they'll say they have no money. Invite them to try new things, and they'll say they have no experience. Tell them to try something new and they'll say they have no expertise.

"You call this a 'poverty mindset,' huh?"

"Accepting we're not worth much. Poverty. Yep. Too many people compare themselves to friends who are as hopeless or stuck as they are. Low bar. They think more than a university professor and do less than a crawling snail. It's as if some sinister marketer has inscribed a tattoo on their souls that says, 'You don't have what it takes. You're not worth much!'

"Gus, if more people would realize who they really are and what they really have to offer, things would change. The key is you have to be motivated by the picture of you in the future. The you leading, learning, loving. And that's exactly what needs to be created today! It's in your soul…. Being able to discern what God is doing in your life and in your spirit."

"Mr. T, I believe you're absolutely right. But you know what it's like. You know you're not living up to your potential. You know you're not killin' it in the areas you know you're gifted in. But what's gonna change anything?"

"Gus, I invest in myself. INVESTING in yourself and in your dreams is vital. People who grow to great heights aren't afraid to put their money and time where their confidence lies. And yet most people don't even read books or attend workshops!

"I recently read a study from a company called the Jenkins group. It said that one-third of high school graduates never read another book for the rest of their lives. Forty-two percent of college graduates don't read a book once they graduate from college. Even if you just read one book a month, or even just listened to one audio book a month, think how far ahead you'd be!"

"How do you decide what books to read, Mr. T?"

"I actually pick a theme for my learning in a year. Then my goal is to become an expert on that topic. One year, it was entrepreneurship. Another year, spiritual growth. One year, it was birds. Then I go about getting books on the subject, videos, audio books, attending talks and seminars. Think of what would happen in your mind if you invested in it with one topic each year.

"Okay, maybe just give it a shot for ninety days. It's actually really fun!"

"All those books and seminars could get expensive."

"Gus, you can find plenty of things out there for free. But when it comes to investing in growth, I think most people would do better to put their money where their desires are. Where their dreams are. Don't just invest time and energy. Invest money.

"Over the years, I've invested many thousands of dollars in my own growth. Actually, hundreds of thousands to tell you the truth. I've paid for live educational seminars, physical trainers, counselors, personal coaching, and even spiritual directors. By investing in myself, I show confidence that my getting to the next level is worthwhile for me, my family, and even the world.

"Gus, have you ever worked with a coach?"

"Sure! Baseball. Track. Basketball. And I'd say my football coach changed my life."

"Why? What did he do?"

"He saw talent in me. He helped me see what I could offer. He challenged me to a higher level. He pulled out of me the hardest work I've ever done and held me accountable. He extracted the best from me."

"And what happened?"

"I won. The team won. It was actually what helped me get a scholarship to play football in college."

"The coach had faith in you, right?" Mr. Turnquest asked.

"Yeah."

"Once you're no longer in high school or college or working for a company that provides good development, then who's responsible to invest in your growth?"

"Me?"

"Yes! I honestly believe the reason many don't invest in themselves is because they have a faith problem. They don't have hope for a great future for themselves. So they stop investing in themselves. They don't intentionally nurture their own growth and they start to rust."

"I think you're right," said Gus. "But why would that be the case?"

"Want to hear what I really think?"

"Isn't that what you always share?"

"Yeah. I guess so! Well, I think that most don't believe in God's ability to be powerful in them and through them—to do much more than get through life, save some money, and hope to retire as young as possible. The stuff we spoke about in the BELIEVING habit.

"But what most really want, when they're honest with themselves, is to fulfill their bigger purposes. But then they're afraid they're nothing all that special. They think of their own talents and abilities and think, 'I'm not that great.' Gus, the key is we all need to practice the Habit of INVESTING, and to do that, we need to believe that we have something special to offer the world. We need the faith that God will take our own measly fishes and loaves and multiply them beyond our wildest dreams to create the influence and impact we can have."

Gus could once again see the passion in Mr. Turnquest's eyes and hear it in his voice. He started to wonder how it could be that in a world that seems to value education, so few invest in themselves in a practical way.

"Gus, you used the word 'extracted' when you spoke about your coach. That's actually a great word. When most people think of education, they miss the value of being extracted. That's what a great coach can do for you. Extract the real you. Extract your vision. Extract your goals. Extract your actions.

"So how about you, Gus? Do you see why investing in yourself matters so much?"

"I hadn't thought about it that way, Mr. T. I see your point. And I admit, I've been pretty lax in that. Maybe a business conference or so…but not much beyond that. I guess I've seen myself as not having the time, or needing to put the money toward the kids' education and their growth. Maybe I've seen investing in myself as selfish."

"Gus, it's completely *not* selfish to invest in your own growth. You're furthering your ability to increase influence in a world where people still go hungry, grow up without love, or fester in inactivity because they don't have meaningful work.

"There are really some I've identified that would make investing in yourself not just a nice option, but mandatory.

"*First thing I challenge people to do in investing in themselves is—* know that God has called you to do something special. And what I mean by that is you know God has a mission for you and wants you to carry it out, whether it's creative or getting a message out or caring about something that God cares deeply about.

"In the Bible, in Ephesians I believe, it says, 'We are God's workmanship. We were put here on this earth to do the things God Himself planned in advance for us to do.'

"Can you see the power of that? God didn't make a mistake when you were made! What you've been given is on purpose! *You*, my friend, are God's handiwork. You're a work of God, the master artist and creator!"

"How do you treat something that's a great work of art?"

"With respect. Care."

"So do you see you've been given a piece of art by God? It's you! So you don't ignore it. Abuse it. Do whatever it takes to make it better and share it.

"I used to think being selfless meant only investing in other people. I would never buy things for my own good. I didn't realize the kind of return on investment that pours out of people who invest in themselves. It's actually an act of trust and faith to believe you're worthwhile enough to pay a counselor to help clear, extract, or even remove the gunk going on and rattling around in your brain. I know the old school I grew up around said it was weakness to pay for help or service from someone else. My generation would reject someone who *needed* a counselor, a coach, a personal trainer.

"One friend even told me, 'I don't need coaches or counselors. I just rely on myself!' I actually laughed out loud when I heard him say that! 'Guess you don't need doctors, dentists, mechanics, or lawyers either?' I said. It's like believing we really can be self-sufficient enough to create life without others!"

"So where would you suggest starting?" asked Gus. "How do you know what you need?"

"Ask yourself these three questions:

"First: What would your life look like if you were unleashed? Fully alive? Fully thriving. List what you come up with.

"Second: What's holding you back from fully living into your God-given potential or purpose at this point? What roadblocks or hurdles do you face?

"Finally: Who or what could help you overcome the obstacles you identified in number two, the things that are holding you back, and how can you engage number one—your full potential?

"Gus, write those on a piece of paper or put them in a journal. Often, the answers emerge when we have the right questions. Ask the right questions and you'll discover the right answers. Or, as the Chinese proverb says, 'He who asks a question is a fool for five minutes; he who does not ask a question remains a fool forever.'"

"Ha! That's good! And those three questions are really powerful!" exclaimed Gus.

"Of course, you may not be able to address or invest in every part of you at once. But those who don't invest in themselves and seek out growth opportunities are destined to end up like that old Ford, Gus.

"When you invest in something, you believe it's going to grow and change and provide a good return on the investment. Invest in what you want to grow. Care for what you want to become better.

"Do you believe you're worthy of investment?"

"Are you asking me?" Gus asked, after an awkward silence.

"Yes."

"I'd like to believe I am," Gus said. "But I've actually taken the path that when I put money or time toward me, I'm actually taking away from my family and their needs."

"Well, you see them as worth the investment, don't you?"

"Sure. We paid for tutors for my son in math and science. You know. Braces. Actually had one of my sons get help from a counselor when he was struggling with school. Paid for a private school."

"And don't you think their dad would be a better dad if he invested in his own growth also?"

"I hear you," said Gus.

"'Love your neighbor as you love yourself!' One very important way to build the hope inside of you is to build the hope inside of you...not accidentally, but totally on purpose! Gus, if you start investing in your own growth as a priority...it *is* going to improve your performance. I see it again and again around Hope. Those who invest become the best!"

"Wow, that's pretty good!" Gus said.

"Invest in you! You're worth it!" Turnquest repeated.

Habit of Hope:
Investing in Yourself and Your Dreams

Summarized: Realize who you really are, what you desire, and what you have to offer. Then invest in your growth and dreams to help you become that real you. Stay motivated by a positive picture of you in the future. Invest money, time, and resources to best succeed in doing what you do best.

Realized: What benefit or benefits might you (and/or others) see or experience by you practicing this habit of *Investing in Yourself and in Your Dreams* as a way of life?

Evaluated: How far along are you in the habit of *Investing in Yourself and in Your Dreams* presently? (1 not at all to 10 completely)

1   2   3   4   5   6   7   8   9   10

Applied: What will you do to practice or grow the habit of *Investing in Yourself and in Your Dreams*?

Habit Releaser:

Gain greater clarity on your vision and picture of a positive and powerful future. Try asking this question: *If God were to bless you and you were free to live into your destiny, what exists five years from now that doesn't exist now?*

Register for a class, training, or further education that will equip you to your next level of growth, expertise, or competence.

Hire a coach, counselor, or consultant to equip or empower you to your next level or walk with you to turn your dream into reality.

CHAPTER 19

TRUSTING: TRUSTING GOD'S RHYTHMS

"Life is ten percent what happens to
me and ninety percent how I react."

— Charles Swindoll

As they walked back, Mr. Turnquest and Gus passed by a stream. Turnquest turned and walked over to the stream, bent down, and picked up a rock.

The stream flowed over rocks, and with the heavier rains over the last few weeks, side tributaries had begun flowing into it. Turnquest stuck his hand in, felt the current, and sloshed some water.

"What are you doing?" asked Gus.

"Oh, just appreciating the stream. Love, love, *love* the sound and the refreshing glow of the sun off the water." He gazed at the stream, breathing in its freshness and listening to its sound as if locked in a trance.

"Why are you doing that?" asked Gus, somewhat perplexed by Mr. Turnquest's ability to just stop and seem enraptured by the things most people just walk by.

"I just love it."

The Need for Kairos

"You don't seem to be in any rush to get places, Mr. T. Don't you have things to do? Where do you find the time to watch a stream flow?"

"Oh, we all have the time, my friend. Time's a real gift—especially the gift of kairos."

"What's that?"

"Kairos, my friend, is one of the world's most undervalued natural gifts. It's actually a Greek word that means the opportune moment. It's the right time. Now. No rush. Fully in the moment. Fully present. Fully right here. Right now. It's the way God acts when it comes to time. Not rushed. Not too busy. Not overbooked. Instead, fully present.

"There's another Greek word for time that's much more common to most of us. It's *chronos*. It's the sequence of moments…tick, tick, tock. Tick tock. Chronos emphasizes the duration of the time. It's where we get the words chronology, chronograph, chronicle.

"For most, time is not their friend. They still have to live in a world where chronos matters. But in Hope, we believe we must trust kairos."

"What do you mean by 'trust kairos'?" questioned Gus.

"Listen to this," said Mr. Turnquest, as he grabbed a piece of paper from his pocket. "It's actually from the Bible.

"Are you tired? Worn out? Burned out on religion? Come to me. Get away with me and you'll recover your life.

"I'll show you how to take a real rest. Walk with me and work with me—watch how I do it. Learn the unforced rhythms of grace. I won't lay anything heavy or ill-fitting on you. Keep company with me and you'll learn to live freely and lightly."

"Wow! That's in the Bible!" Gus said.

"It's actually from a version called *The Message*. It's an interpretation of Matthew 11:28-30.

"Fear gets inside us, and over time, it just tires our souls. Drains us. It tires us at a level no typical rest can restore. Like a battery that's been drained by running the lights all night long, it's lost its charge. The only way to get back the soul's energy when it's been depleted by times and seasons of fear is to surrender to the unforced rhythms of grace. Trusting in kairos and not rushing everything. Eliminating fear from our daily schedules.

"And how often is fear really at the root of stress, striving, and hurry? Gus, you must eliminate hurry from your life in the same way a doctor cuts out a cancerous growth."

"So how much hurry must I remove?" Gus asked.

"Ha! All of it!" he said, smiling. "You must eliminate all of it. Leave none. Zero. Nada. Actually, when you trust in God's rhythms of grace, God replaces hurry in your life. You'll start to notice when you're letting hurry lead, and then you're job is to surrender it."

"Does that apply in things like business too?"

"Especially business! Work hard, of course, but also by trusting the rhythms of grace, not in rushing, and without pushing and controlling. That's actually what kills business! Whenever you catch yourself in a hurry, know this: that's not living in hope. That's not the unforced rhythm of grace.

"The Habit of TRUSTING God's unforced rhythms means we let go and believe there's an appointed time for everything. Winter turns to spring, turns to summer, turns to fall.... No need to rush it here in the Adirondacks. It just happens naturally. Trust there is a time for 'every season under heaven.'

"Ever watched a butterfly leaving a cocoon?"

"No. Have you?" Gus asked.

"Yes. It's God-ordained genius. And it takes time. Do you know what happens when you seek to rush the butterfly out of the cocoon?"

"I've heard it dies," said Gus.

"That's right. Rush things before their time and you can kill them. Try to become an overnight success, an instant millionaire, or build fast relationships, and guess what? You kill them. Did you know that many men beyond their twenties these days have only one or even no close friendships with other guys. Can you think of why that might be?"

"No time?" said Gus.

"Exactly. Remember how friendships formed when you were a kid or even a teen. You hung out. You shot the breeze. But then guys find themselves so *busy* working, taking care of business, or earning a living that they forget to take the time to earn a life…. They forget that most of the best things in life take the willingness to trust *kairos*…. Live in the unforced rhythms of grace…in *kairos*. Look at that leaf flowing down the little stream. Do you think it's working hard? Checking time. Multi-tasking? No. It's just going with the flow. It's being…not doing.

"Gus, we in Hope make it our aim to eliminate hurry from our lives."

"All of it, huh?"

"Yes, all the hurry!" Mr. Turnquest said. "Sure, emergencies come up. But mostly, we hurry out of fear. Hurry does not come from faith. So when you experience typical hurry, ask yourself, 'Am I afraid of something?' Then what I do is say a prayer."

"What kind of prayer?" Gus asked.

"I love the Serenity Prayer:

> God, grant me the serenity to accept the things I cannot change,
>
> Courage to change the things I can,

211

And wisdom to know the difference.

Living one day at a time; enjoying one moment at a time."

"I love that," said Gus. "That's powerful."

"I also sometimes just take what I call a release break," Mr. Turnquest said.

"What's that?"

"TRUSTING God's Rhythms as a habit means I break from my work or whatever I'm doing periodically. I close my eyes, and just prayerfully breathe in, then breathe out, and say 'Release.' I say it either silently or sometimes out loud. It's my way of giving God back the control. I'm releasing the stuff I'm fearing. I'm releasing the toxins I've taken in."

"I love that too!" Gus said, feeling like he'd just discovered a new gem.

"A life of hurry brings disorder to our souls. The TRUSTING God's Rhythms Habit makes us release our own inner hustle that won't ever force everything to behave the way we want it to. In reality, the try harder stuff typically wastes more than it gains."

"I guess it's like what athletes learn. There's a time to train and a time to rest. Work the muscle. Rest the muscle."

"Yes! Great creative acts, Gus—do most of them come from hurry?"

"No. Of course not. They come from peace. They come from taking the time to consider. Reflect. Being human beings, not human doings."

"Yes. We're human beings, not human doings. Gus, trusting God's rhythms and accepting God's kairos means trusting two things. One: There is a God. Two: I'm not Him.

"When we let our lives get frantic, fast-paced, hurried, it creates consistent fight-or-flight stress that our bodies and souls weren't meant to handle. It may just mean we don't believe either God exists or we are not God. Or a mix!

"None of us escapes the great lie that we can rush life. Nature illustrates this so perfectly. Seasons change in time. Streams flow consistently. They don't rush. Leaves turn color in time."

"Unforced rhythms of grace," said Gus.

"Yes! How much anxiety and loss of hope springs from our unwillingness to lean into that unforced rhythm of grace?

"The prophet Isaiah wrote, 'But those who hope in the Lord will renew their strength. They will soar on wings like eagles; they will run and not grow weary, they will walk and not be faint.' That's the activity of Hope, Gus. It's allowing God's timing to create the best things. When we remain hopeful, despite our waiting, God rewards us with interior strength, letting us enjoy the journey instead of rushing it.

The "Yet Mindset"

"Have you ever heard of the 'Yet Mindset?'" Turnquest asked.

"No. Not yet, I guess!"

"Well, that's kind of it. It's the lie that something will never happen because it hasn't happened *yet*. If you're not happy *yet*, it will never happen. If you don't have a happy marriage *yet*, it will never happen. If you don't love your job *yet*, you will never love it.

"The TRUSTING God's Rhythms habit requires faith. *Yet* doesn't mean *never*—or not even soon. How many stories of those who quit too soon do we need to hear to realize that persisting in hope and taking our time matters?

"You haven't struck gold…*yet*.

"You haven't grown your business to meet your goal…*yet*."

"The Resistance to Trust loves the lie that if it hasn't happened yet, it never will! The evil one so wants you to quit. I have no doubt that many marriages, which would have been great, end in divorce by quitting too soon. The evil one whispers, 'You're not gonna make it! You've been trying for a long time! You'll never change! They'll never change!'

"Gus, God's *made everything beautiful in its time*, as it says in Ecclesiastes. That was written by the wisest man in the world, Solomon. Sure you long for it now, and that's good and bad. God wants to see you succeed in life even more than you do! But God's not going to force-grow you! God's not going to force-feed you! Instead, as you relax and live into God's incredible timing, you'll get to see that things really do become beautiful in their time.

"Do you know why you're here in Hope now, Gus?"

"Well, if I hear you correctly, this was my time."

"*Yes*! That's exactly the point. Timing. You're here now because this is your time to learn *The Habits of Hope*. Had you heard these things five years ago, you probably wouldn't have been ready. And you do know what one of the greatest motivators to engage real hope is, right?"

"Pain?"

"You got that right!" Turnquest exclaimed. "If you hadn't been through the gunk, the mud, and the crap, you'd think you didn't need anything else. But you'd be missing out on the best life has to offer. *'The Lord is good to those who hope in him.'* The spiritual person is the person who doesn't force it. That person waits on God. He or she trusts God's unforced rhythms of grace.

"Jesus taught something that's so counter-intuitive to a get-it-now, instant gratification world that it almost seems silly and quaint to most people. It's what I shared before. 'Seek first the Kingdom of God and his righteousness. And all these things shall be added unto you.'

The Most Productive Thing We Can Do

"Often the greatest and most productive thing we can do in our day is to seek God. Pray. Wait on God's open door. God's answer. That applies to business. That applies to marriages gone astray. Even kids gone astray! Do you know the story of the prodigal son, Gus?"

"Basically," said Gus. "Son gets his inheritance and heads out. He parties and loses everything. Then when he shows up back at home, his father welcomes him. I think he even runs to greet him."

"Exactly! And the whole time the son is away, what does the father do? He waits! He doesn't force the timing. He doesn't force his son. That's how God operates. God is patient. God doesn't force us. And we can do the same.

"Timing, Gus. Timing. TRUSTING God's Rhythms. Every single day. God won't be rushed. God's timing is perfect. Perfect."

After a full day of wisdom and learning these life-giving habits, Mr. Turnquest brought Gus to his room, and left him there to settle in for the night. Gus' head was full with all he had learned during the day. But it didn't feel like a heavy load. Instead, it felt light. Freeing.

"Where have these habits been all my life?" Gus thought. "So many wasted days could have been saved had I known this! So much pain avoided!"

Then, almost instantly, he heard loud and clear in Mr. Turnquest's voice: "God's timing is perfect. Perfect."

Gus knew the timing of this message and the explanation of this habit, "TRUSTING God's Unforced Rhythms" was right for him. Today had been the day he needed to hear this message. Now was the time to trust.

It was also the time to get some sleep.

That night, Gus slept more restfully and deeply than he had in quite a long time. *Maybe* there was a connection.

Habit of Hope:
Trusting God's Rhythms

Summarized: Trust in God's unforced rhythms in the world and experience "kairos" by intentionally taking breaks from your work or whatever you feel compelled to do periodically. Allow yourself to enjoy each moment fully and be okay with things not all being perfect or realized yet. Let go of the need to be in control of all the outcomes.

Realized: What benefit or benefits might you (and/or others) see or experience by you practicing this habit as a way of life?

Evaluated: How far along are you in the habit of *Trusting God's Rhythms* presently? (1 not at all to 10 completely)

1   2   3   4   5   6   7   8   9   10

Applied: What will you do to practice or grow the habit of *Trusting God's Rhythms*?

Habit Releaser:

Create times of sabbath (a restful break) in your week as a regular practice. Do things that are not in your area of work and that refresh your mind, body, and soul.

Take walks during the day. Even if it's fifteen minutes or a half an hour, get outside and appreciate the "unforced rhythms" of nature and life. Look around at nature. Look up at the sky.

Insert "yet" into more sentences that involve your deepest desires. "I'm not married *yet*." "I don't own my dream home *yet*." "We're not out of debt *yet*."

Pray the serenity prayer when you feel anxious or stressed over something. "God, grant me the serenity to accept the things I cannot change...."

CHAPTER 20

SURROUNDING: SURROUNDING YOURSELF WITH POSITIVE PEOPLE

"Alone we can do so little; together we can do so much."

— Helen Keller

The morning mist silently rose over the lake as Gus and Mr. Turnquest walked over to the beach. A band of ducks scurried off and scooted across the water as the men made their way through dew-drenched sand. Gus still had no idea why they were up so early and what was important enough to make him leave the warmth of his bed and immerse himself in the early morning cold.

Suddenly, out of the mist, the stillness cracked with the rev of an engine. A powerful eight-cylinder inboard engine roared to life, startling both men.

"Rodney, is that you?" shouted a strangely familiar voice from the back of the boat.

Through the mist, the figure of a tall, slender man emerged, wrapping a tow line as he advanced. He was a middle-aged man with a receding hairline, but an athletic build—ripped abs and bulging pecs. He was wearing a tight-fitting, dark blue wetsuit, and had the bearing of someone who had just won the lottery.

"Yep, it sure is, Benn!" Turnquest shouted back.

"It's perfect out here! And we've got the whole lake to ourselves... even if we can hardly see a thing! Bob and Rich are on their way over to join us. And, of course, Todd's up first!" Benn said.

"Great! This is my friend, Gus."

"Hey, Gus! Nice to meet you. Are you gonna ski?"

"Skiing in October? Not a chance!" Gus said, laughing. "You guys are nuts!"

"That's the fun of it, Gus! Todd is the nuttiest of us. He's already in the water. But ya gotta admit, it's pretty perfect out here. Lake's like glass! Pure. Cold. Glass!"

"Mornin', Todd!" Turnquest shouted. "I want you to meet my friend, Gus."

"Mornin', Gus! You gonna ski?" Todd asked, treading water.

"Wasn't planning on it, Todd!" Gus said.

"Gonna be awesome out here, Gus. Do you ski?" Todd asked.

"Yeah. But it's been a while. And freezing to death doesn't seem to be the best way of starting a day. Besides, I tried that the other night."

"I hear you," said Todd, not understanding Gus' allusion to the other night. "Lisa convinced me the water's warmer than the air. You'll never feel a thing once you get moving! Not even your hands—ever again!" Todd laughed.

As they were talking, Rich, Lisa and Bob pulled into the dock.

"Mornin', guys!" shouted Lisa from the boat as she jumped out and grabbed a rope. "Glass this morning! Total glass! Just can't see much."

"Except for your big honkin' wake ruining it!" Benn said, smiling. "All right, folks, you're here. At least join us in the boat."

"I'm in!" Turnquest said.

"Why not?" Gus agreed.

And with that, the men climbed into the late model Ski Nautique and joined the crew.

Bob drove and Todd skied first. Rich manned the ropes.

"Go!" Todd shouted, as he threw the rope's slack into the water, hopped once, and was instantly standing on his slalom ski, racing over the glassy water as the boat gunned forward.

Todd's skiing was flawless as he cut rapidly back and forth, practically touching his shoulders to the water on each pass, kicking up awesome fantails.

"The guy's amazing!" shouted Rich above the sound of the boat. "I never get tired of watching him ski!"

"Wanna ski next, Gus?" asked Lisa, not realizing Gus had already declined more than once.

"No thanks. I'm just enjoying watching you guys," said Gus.

"You sure?" said Lisa. "Doesn't get any better than this."

"I'm good."

Gus and Mr. Turnquest watched as the others took turns, each rooting for the skier and congratulating them on their skills and overcoming the cold.

After Benn skied, the sun began cutting through the mist, and just a hint of warmth began radiating from the water.

"You're certainly welcome to use my ski if you want to go, Gus," said Bob.

"What the heck!" said Gus. "Why not?"

Turnquest grinned. "Yer not gonna regret it, Partner!"

"You want to wear my wetsuit?" offered Todd.

"Well…yeah! I know how cold this water can be," said Gus,

remembering his recent brush with the lake. It kind of seemed now like it had just been a bad dream. "Sure!"

Within minutes, Gus was wearing the pre-moistened suit and was in the water. Rich threw him the rope, and moments later, Gus was cutting through the water, smiling. He couldn't believe it! To his own surprise, he hadn't forgotten how to ski—he hadn't forgotten how to cut, jump the wake, or feel incredibly alive while doing it!

Without a fall, Gus finished and sliced into the shallow water off the sandy beach as he let go of the rope.

"Rodney told us you hadn't skied in years! Did you lie to him?" jibed Bob.

Turnquest climbed from the boat onto the dock and joined Gus on the beach.

"Great skiing, Partner!"

"Yeah, thanks! I'm gonna be sore, but that was pretty amazing! So glad I did that!"

"What made you do it, Gus?"

"Foolishness? Or was it a bunch of awesome people having a blast together? I guess they wore me down!"

"And that's the next habit of Hope, Gus! Exactly!"

"What, exactly?" asked Gus.

Surround Yourself with Hopeful People

"You couldn't help but become part of their party! Here in Hope, we believe hope is contagious. So we intentionally surround ourselves with people who can encourage, challenge, and see the best in us. SURROUND yourself with hopeful and positive people. Let me tell you, getting isolated is a sure way to stay where you are. Stuck.

"Have you ever heard of 'The Vagabonds,' Gus?"

"No, can't say I have. Wait—were they a punk band?"

"Ha!" Turnquest said. "No, not quite! The Vagabonds was the name given to a group of men who decided they could inspire each other to even greater things. Ever heard of Henry Ford? Thomas Edison? Harvey Firestone? John Burroughs?"

"Of course," said Gus.

"Well, starting in about 1915, and for the next ten years, these 'Four Vagabonds' embarked on a series of summer camping trips. They came here to the Adirondacks, went to the Green Mountains, Upper Michigan, and caravanned to mountains in West Virginia, Tennessee, and North Carolina.

"I've heard that at least once, President Harding even joined them. And at campsites, Ford would challenge his fellow adventurers to contests involving everything from high kicking to tree chopping. Can you imagine, the President, Warren Harding, doing high kicks with Edison? I'd like to post that video online!

"Ford encouraged Edison to learn birdcalls and identify flowers. I like that guy! These guys had a blast together!

"Why do I share this, Gus? Because we all need our band of vagabonds! We need to SURROUND ourselves with hopeful people. Find our own positive and powerful people who won't let us settle for sitting on the sidelines and will keep us growing in hope.

"Don't you think these vagabonds were *too busy* to do all that traveling? Of course! But they were too smart to go without their band of brothers. These 'too busy guys' would sit around a fire and talk about their visions and dreams. Edison would intentionally share his chemical formulas, and they would debate current topics and challenge each other's thinking and creativity.

"Let me highlight the word 'intentionally.' If you don't *intentionally* surround yourself with others who have hopes and dreams, you'll isolate yourself from the fire and the fuel of creativity."

Become Part of a Positive Group

"Who are your positive and powerful men and women?" Turnquest asked.

"Well, my friend Brian and I grab lunch once in a while. My brother-in- law Mike's pretty awesome. We go fishing once every few years. But, as I've gotten older, I don't think I've got any kind of positive group or vagabond types. I think I need that."

"Get them together then! Or intentionally become part of some kind of a vagabond, cohort, or mastermind group where you surround yourself with others with dreams and visions. Positive people.

"Not only does this intentional surrounding increase the fun factor, but it increases your positive thoughts. It increases your ability to take action when you'd rather sit on the shore. You need those who can challenge you to hope!"

"I've heard the term," said Gus, "but what exactly is a MasterMind group, Mr. Turnquest?"

"A MasterMind is a group of people who come together to hold each other accountable to their goals, to help each other solve problems, and to come up with ideas. I see it as my own personal board of advisors, in a way. It's about business, but it's also very much connected to my personal and spiritual life. It's really hard to separate that out.

"Every Friday morning, I meet with Al, Pete, Sam, Alice, and Joe. Joe's the facilitator. We drink plenty of coffee at Common Grounds Cafe and we share what we're doing. We're coming up on three years together soon. When we can't meet in person, we do it virtually.

"Sometimes, we read books together. Often we do a 'hot seat' and help someone with a problem. Then every quarter or so, we do a retreat together. And we do it at someone's cabin. We've gone camping. Fishing. In the winter, snowmobiling, downhill skiing, or cross country skiing," Mr. Turnquest said.

"If it's the right group. Right leadership. Right vision of really helping each other succeed and live with purpose and meet our goals, such a group is worth its weight in gold! How much could it be worth in your life and business if you had a group that believed in the best you and wouldn't let you fail?

"I think most people do themselves a disservice by not investing in their growth in this way! I see that as similar to the INVESTING Habit. Just like this group of water-ski vagabonds, our Friday morning a group pushes each other to be the best we can possibly be! And that builds hope. And together, we build Hope...if you know what I mean!"

"Gus, when you find your complements, you just don't need to go it alone or be a one-man band. Find your tribe! Invest in them and *surround* yourself with hopeful people. Then stick with them!" Turnquest concluded.

Habit of Hope:

Surrounding Yourself with Positive People

Summarized: Find other hopeful or positive people who become part of a group who won't let each other settle for mediocrity or negativity. Join or create positive or MasterMind groups where together you do more than any one of you could do isolated or alone.

Realized: What benefit or benefits might you (and/or others) see or experience by your practicing this habit of *Surrounding Yourself with Positive People* as a way of life?

Evaluated: How far along are you in this habit of *Surrounding Yourself with Positive People* presently? (1 not at all to 10 completely)

1   2   3   4   5   6   7   8   9   10

Applied: What will you do to practice or grow this habit of *Surrounding Yourself with Positive People?*

Habit Releaser:

Make a list of the positive or growth-oriented people in your community or relationships (or at least those whom you sense hunger for that kind of hope-filled life and leadership).

Create a lunch, breakfast, or coffee meeting for your positive group. If it's positive and encouraging, do it again!

Apply for and/or join a business group, cohort, or MasterMind of other like-minded people in your field of similar endeavor. (At least give it a try and see whether it is a fit. Not all groups are the same quality. Look for one that fits you.) It may be in person, virtual, or a mix of both.

CHAPTER 21

OFFERING: OFFERING YOUR GIFTS GENEROUSLY

"Hide not your talents. They for use were made.
What's a sundial in the shade?"

— Benjamin Franklin

G us and Mr. Turnquest left the beach and headed into town to the Common Grounds Cafe which Mr. Turnquest said had some of the best coffee and omelets in the world.

Soon after sitting down, Mr. Turnquest was greeted warmly by two of the waitresses, who hugged him enthusiastically.

"This is my friend, Gus," Mr. Turnquest told them. "He's from out of town, and he's checking out Hope."

"Welcome to Hope!" both women chimed at the same time.

"Welcome to Common Grounds Cafe! Glad you've joined us," said the twenty-something with the name Jamie embroidered on her blouse.

"This is Jamie. And this is Lisa, Gus. They're the best waitresses and cafe owners around! They started this place a few years back. Great entrepreneurs. They run this place and even do some real estate investing on the side."

Within moments, Jamie brought the two men breakfast menus and poured them both cups of steaming hot coffee.

"The service here is incredible! Actually, I might say, the service in Hope is incredible everywhere!"

"I've already experienced that! It's like these people all love helping or something!" Gus said. "In some ways, it's creepy. Maybe because it's not typical! Actually more wonderful, though. Like people around here really seem excited about their work! Service."

"They do! Does that surprise you?"

"Well, I've definitely encountered good service here and there. But not from everywhere! And not with such sincerity!"

"Yeah, it took us time and effort, but all of us in Hope practice the Habit of OFFERING our gifts generously. You see, Jamie and Lisa don't work for money."

"They work for free?" Gus asked, surprised.

"Ha," Mr. Turnquest laughed. "I should say they work for more than money. They get paid. Actually, the tips here are incredible! But that's not why they work. They work because they love what they do and they offer their gifts each day in and through their work."

"Mr. Turnquest, where I come from most people seem more disengaged when it comes to their work. Most can't wait until Friday or the weekend!"

"And that's where the Habits of Hope create measurable change. That's the status quo for too many people where you're from. It definitely doesn't need to be that way. This habit can transform your work and your play. Maybe even make your work feel more like play!"

"Okay, so how? **Work feel more like play?** You've got my attention."

Grow Hope by Generously Offering What You're Meant to Give

"We call this the Habit of Hope of OFFERING Your Gifts Generously and it means we do what we do as acts of service. We see the work we do as giving, not only receiving. Have you ever just worked for a paycheck, Gus?"

"Yeah. Just about every day! It's almost impossible for me to imagine anything else."

"Who taught you that you should work for a paycheck?"

"I don't know. My dad. Well, maybe just everyone. Don't most people work for a paycheck?"

"Nothing wrong with a paycheck for sure. But, when you're feeling drained, empty, or disconnected from your work, there's something wrong. It could be your fault, but Hope doesn't work that way.

"What would you do if you didn't need to get paid? I mean, what would you do to benefit other people?"

"You know, I think that feels so distant from my life, or way of thinking, I almost don't know any more. It almost seems impractical. Not real life."

"Yet that's the realest life. You were created with something to bring to the world that makes a difference."

"Sounds pretty optimistic. How do you know what you should give?"

Jamie returned and cheerfully asked the two men for their orders as she topped off their coffee. Turnquest opted for his typical "Egg White Scramble" filled with spinach, tomatoes and feta cheese. Gus ordered the "Western Omelet" with ham, cheddar, green pepper and onions. The whole place smelled of Adirondack breakfast awesomeness.

"In Hope, we don't just put people through school and then encourage them to get a job to earn a paycheck," said Mr. Turnquest returning to the conversation.

"What do you do then?"

"We help them discover the gifts, passions, skills, and deepest desires in themselves. It's what we call 'convergence.' And it all starts with excavating people's gifts on purpose."

"How does that work?" asked Gus. "Can you know when you're in the right place or not?"

Excavating Your Gifts On Purpose

"Well, the Bible for starters. The Bible is clear God didn't make people randomly. God was intentional. The Psalms say a person is 'knit together in their mother's womb.' My version says we're 'fearfully and wonderfully made.'

"'Truth is: You've never met an accidental person. You're no accidental person. You were knit together by God himself. And what you've been given are gifts. And you're a steward of the gifts God's given you. And that affects the way we educate and equip our people in Hope."

"How?"

"It has to! Great education helps people find their own path, then follow it. You can't educate everyone the same way since God didn't create just one model or give one set of gifts.

"If you believe people each have unique gifts, talents, and abilities, it makes no sense to just train them in a one-size-fits-all way. Don't educate them to be like others and expect them to perform the same way on some standardized testing. Or even find their major without guidance. Yet, that's how so much education outside of Hope treats people. It's as if they're nothing but wet cement with no inherent design."

"How do you train people here?"

"Good question. Well, as you know, the Bible wasn't written in English, right? So in Proverbs 22:6, the best translation from the original Hebrew says "Train up a youth according to his bent." In other words, help each kid to understand "his way." Don't force him into some random way of doing work. Help him find his bent.

Help him discover and engage in what he was created to do—authentically express his gifts in the world. His work.

"No child is deposited into our care at birth without a prescribed set of characteristics or bents.

"The key Hebrew word in the Proverb is *derek*, or 'way.' So even your work can be an authentic out-flowing of your real identity. And convergence happens when you're guided, then encouraged to fully express your bent in your work in the world."

"Wow! That's so missing in most educational settings where I come from," agreed Gus. "And then we wonder why so many hate their jobs, feel stuck, or become disengaged. There would be a lot of benefits to that!"

"Well, there's education. And then there's excavation. Empowering a person to be their best requires both. And excavation is key to education. And vice versa. We need both."

"What's the difference?"

"Education imparts information and helps you learn how to think. It teaches you by giving you what you don't have. Excavation, on the other hand, brings out what you already have. Your bent for one. It gets at what's inside you. How you tick. Helps you see what you have to offer."

"How do you excavate a person?"

"It's mostly about asking probing questions that unlock the real them. Great questions draw out the gold trapped inside in deep veins under the ground. The gold exists inside every person ever created. But when it's excavated and brought to the surface, that's when the magic happens. That's when you see how you're an emissary of good. You know your bigger purpose. That's when you feel the courage and the confidence to express your gold without holding back. And the results: a whole lot of hope gets released."

"What does the excavation process look for?"

Experiencing Convergence of Your Passions, Proficiencies, and Platform

"Well, excavation aims to discover and engage three keys to hope-filled life and work: your authentic passions. Your truest proficiencies. And the best platform to use them. And when all three come together, that's when *convergence* happens. That's when you're at your best.

"I know some think it's naive to believe you can just do what you're passionate about. And to a certain extent, I agree. That's true. Just because you're passionate about it doesn't mean you're good at it."

"Yeah. Like, I love music. And I'm tone deaf!"

"Ha! Totally! And I'm convinced that in a world where upwards of 70 percent of people say they're disengaged from their work or wish they could do something else, a lot of hope gets drained every single day between nine to five. A lot of hope gets lost on the job!

"But on the contrary, the habit of OFFERING Your Gifts Generously encourages each of us to know our gifts and use them. We gain more energy than we lose."

"Can you know those three things for sure? Your passion, for example?" questioned Gus.

"Well, what do you think passion is?"

"I would say passion is when you get fired up about something? You care. It means something to you."

"Good definition. I agree. So why not intentionally know what you have to offer? Gain clarity and do more of it. Say 'No' to what's not you.

"First, Excavate Passion?" said Turnquest. "What makes you pound a fist on a table? What bugs you? Or what touches your heart or brings tears to your eyes? When passion is present, you experience drive. You're motivated. You're inspired to act."

"Answer those questions. Then start seeking ways to offer your passions as a way of life. It's possible that you navigate to areas of your passion. But, why not take time to be intentional? Then be a steward of your own passion."

"And you see proficiencies as complementing that?"

"Very much so. Passion and proficiencies together are like a dynamic duo in a person. Your proficiencies aren't an accident either. Some proficiencies are developed by training. Others, you've just had since you were a kid as an expression of how God wired you. You may not even know your proficiencies. It's possible to become blind to our own real proficiencies.

"Next, Excavate Proficiencies: What gifts, strengths, and abilities do you have? What are you doing when you lose all track of time or feel fully absorbed or in the zone? My own coach, Diane, says you should explore the times in your life when you are 'on track.' When do you feel like you're just doing what you're made to do?

"Finally, Excavate Platform: Where's your best place, or what's the best kind of organization you come alive in? How do you work with other people to do more together than apart? Do you work best as a freelancer or as a team member? Are you an influencer or team leader or better as a supporter? Do you thrive by being part of a small team? Or a large organization? Do you manage other people, or would you rather be a technician, a doer?

At that moment, Jamie placed the steaming hot breakfast plates, creatively garnished, in front of the two. They both thanked her and, after Turnquest said a short prayer of thanks to God, they began to eat.

Expressing Your Gifts to Solve Problems

As the two ate, Gus said, "It makes total sense to be intentional about knowing and using your gifts and passions. Excavating them. Even finding the best platform to do that. But, honestly, I can be pretty selfish. In a perfect world, everyone would serve others with all their gifts and passions. Frankly, sometimes I just think, 'What's in it for me?'"

"I totally appreciate that," said Turnquest. "I can relate. And I know we are not alone one bit! It's part of being human to ask 'What's in it for me?' and 'If I'm generous with my gifts, then what?'

"Lisa, can you come over here for a second," motioned Turnquest.

"Sure. How can I help you, Rodney?" asked Lisa walking toward the table.

"You own The Common Grounds. Why do you run this place?"

"Interesting question. Hmmm…a few reasons for sure. First, I'm gifted in hospitality and I'm really good at creating places where people feel welcome and get to connect with each other over great food."

"And the second reason?" ——

"People need this kind of place around here. People need places to connect and build relationships. Awesome food too!"

"Any other reasons?"

"Well, it's how I help support my family. I get paid. You know, money."

"Thanks, Lisa."

"That's it, Rodney?"

"Yep."

"So, you see, Gus, Lisa's solving the three problems. A problem of wanting to be a steward of her own gifts and passions. Then there's the problem others have: They need places to connect. Good food. Hospitality. There's a lot of hope created when people have a common ground experience.

"The third: she gets paid. Actually, in Hope, we pay people well."

"Too many people forget that it's a both-and when it comes to offering their gifts. You can solve a few problems and get paid to solve them. But in Hope we intentionally make the connection to other people's problems that businesses and work solve: shelter, food, clothing, health care, relaxation, personal growth. Jobs. You name it.

"And God is in the business of solving problems by creating gifted people with passions, proficiencies, and platforms.

"Why do you think business exists in the first place?"

"Well, I would think to make a profit. Make things people can buy. Build the economy. Provide jobs. I've never really asked that question."

"All true. However, the bigger reason business exists is just this: human flourishing. Create more human flourishing. Shalom, which means peace in Hebrew. Peace on earth. If Jesus said that his mission was to help people have life, and have it to the full, can you see that applies to us as well?"

"So you see business as helping people have life to the full?"

"Yes! Business and work is God's way of solving problems and creating meaning in everyday life."

"And how does that apply to Offering Gifts generously?"

"You just gotta know what problem or problems you're meant to solve and how your gifts fit. This brings tangible meaning to everyday work!"

"And."

"And what?"

"And you get paid. Not selfish. When you provide real value, steward your gifts, and solve real problems, you should get paid. Get paid well!"

Enjoy Freedom By Offering Generously

"Why do you call this habit '*offering*,' Mr. T?" Gus asked. "It seems like it's about *unearthing* or *excavating. Solving problems.*"

"Because once people's gifts are excavated and they discover the problems they can solve in their work, they practice the habit of OFFERING their gifts generously—giving what they've been given. Nothing more. Nothing less. Nothing else.

"In the Bible, Paul said, '*Therefore, I urge you, in view of God's mercy, to offer your bodies as a living sacrifice.... This is your spiritual act of proper worship.*'

"Offering is not a burden or chore. It's a response. And your work is your worship. You get to worship God by doing what you were born to do day to day. You get to see others thrive and spread hope.

"The truth I've learned the hard way, Gus, is that we only really receive what we give away. When we offer ourselves, that's when we get our real selves. When we offer our own unique gifts as part of God's bigger purpose in the world, that's when we find life.

"As the adage goes, 'Those who lose their life will find it.' God's smart that way. It's really the way the universe works. Things that people hoard get stolen or broken. Eat more and you expend more; you gain fat, not muscle, and over time you become unhealthy.

"A healthy cell offers…then receives.

"Work's not a bad thing! It's actually a good thing! But get clear on what gift you should offer! If you offer something you don't have, you create a deficit.

"It's always an act of faith when you give something away. By doing so, you trust God is good and will provide again tomorrow. And when you offer your gifts to others, you trust you won't expend more than you have to give. Of course, this doesn't work when you are forced or commanded. In 2 Corinthians, it says, 'Give, not under compulsion. Give cheerfully. God loves a cheerful giver.' If you can't do it cheerfully, don't do it…or don't do it yet.

"You want to feel God's love? Then give! Offer! Share!" Turnquest concluded, just as Jamie came to clean up the breakfast plates and the two paid her for breakfast.

"OFFERING your gifts generously creates the best kind of economy—the kind we all want to be part of! That's the path to true wealth in Hope! Practice it!" Mr. Turnquest exclaimed.

"It just may be your time to find or more precisely hone your real gifts. Excavate your passions. Your proficiencies. Your platform. Then solve the problems you were born to solve and create human flourishing and hope for others.

Habit of Hope:
Offering Your Gifts Generously

Summarized: Intentionally experience and express the convergence of your passions, proficiencies, and platform to utilize them. Educate and excavate your gifts. Then be a good steward of them as you use them to benefit other people and enjoy the fulfillment and freedom that comes by offering your authentic gifts out of joy and generosity.

Realized: What benefit or benefits might you (and/or others) see or experience by you practicing the habit of *Offering Your Gifts Generously* as a way of life?

Evaluated: How far along are you in the habit of *Offering Your Gifts Generously* presently? (1 not at all to 10 completely)

1   2   3   4   5   6   7   8   9   10

Applied: What will you do to practice or grow the habit of *Offering Your Gifts Generously*?

246

Habit Releaser:

Excavate your passions: What makes you get really excited? What brings tears to your eyes?

Excavate your proficiencies: Since you were a child, what were you doing when you felt really "on track" or fully in the zone of what you were great at?

Excavate your platform: In what environment(s) do you thrive? What role do you best play and with whom?

Clarify: If you didn't or couldn't use your gifts, what problem would go unsolved or needs would go unmet in the world?

Work with a trained coach to fully excavate and unleash your gifs and empower you to use them in the place you can thrive.

Experiment with some opportunities or new places to use your gifts. Then evaluate. How did it go?

CHAPTER 22

FUELING:
FUELING YOUR BRAIN

"The mind is not a vessel to be filled, but a fire to be kindled."

— Plutarch

T he two men finished their breakfast at Common Grounds, thanked their servers, and tipped them generously, then headed down Hope's Main Street toward the lake.

"Are you ready to talk about another Habit of Hope?" asked Mr. Turnquest.

"Why not! Bring it on!"

"This habit's a bit different. The first ones were very spiritual and more about the inner journey of Hope. This one begins some of the outer journey that affects the inner journey. We call it the habit of FUELING Your Brain."

"Interesting! And why is that a Habit of Hope?"

"So many of us are taught that things like IQ and education are really important. And I'm not diminishing that aspect of education. It matters. But too few of us were even taught how to care for and empower the most important organ in our body—our brain.

"Ever heard of the physicist Michio Kaku?"

"Don't think so."

"Smart guy. He says the human brain has 100 billion neurons, each neuron connected to 10 thousand other neurons. Sitting on your shoulders is the most complicated object in the known universe.'

"100 billion neurons! Incredible! Hard to fathom," said Gus.

"It's only about 2 percent of your body's weight. Yet your brain gobbles up about 20 percent of its energy every day. Brain science is really applicable science. By understanding how to better care for our brains, we end up dramatically increasing the quality and quantity of our lives."

"That makes sense. You see, I'm using my brain."

"When you don't take care of your brain, you diminish your potential for most things.

"In Hope, we realized there were things we did that just didn't seem to help us function at our best. For example:

- Sitting at a desk for eight hours a day.

- Getting anything less than 7 or 8 hours of healthy sleep.

- Not doing something each day that actively uses the parts of our brain that foster creativity.

- Eating foods that give a quick jolt of glucose, but cause grumpiness soon after.

"How you treat your brain each day affects your ability to stay hopeful and happy. Just does!

"We simply must ask ourselves the question: Is doing this good for my brain, or bad for my brain?"

Fuel Your Brain's Recreational Movement

The two men walked along the wooden bridge that led through the woods and offered spectacular views of Hope Mountain. There were exercise instructions at numbered stations along the way, filled with people of all ages doing stretches, squats, pushups, pull-ups, and planks.

"We weren't created to be sedentary and still for most of the day. Our bodies function best when they're moving miles, not just feet between our office and the restroom. For millennia, humans walked everywhere, hunted, and farmed. Do you think that suddenly spending days sitting at 'cubaclized' desks became good for us?"

"No! Not at all. I think being forced to sit at a desk without breaks ruins us physically, and it definitely hinders creativity."

"Just pay attention to your own positivity and hope during and after climbing a mountain. The blood pumping and the oxygen being delivered into your brain energizes your cells.

"Have you ever heard of Jack LaLanne?"

"Of course," said Gus. "I used to go to a health club named after him. He was the king of health and fitness for years."

"You got it! Jack lived to ninety-six, and he stayed totally alert and with it and had the energy of a twenty-year-old."

"Yeah, I heard they named the 'jumping jack' after the guy! And on his seventieth birthday, he towed seventy boats behind him for 1.5 miles in Long Beach Harbor in California."

"Exactly! And the man was still a human! But he did what most don't do. He fostered his own health every single day…and that started with what he did for his brain."

"Moving's so underrated as a habit," said Gus. "Yet, as all the stuff in life increases, it's one of the first things to go. When I get home from work, I'm tired and spent."

"People in Hope shoot to move five miles a day."

"You're kidding! Five?"

"Move at least five miles a day and see what happens inside your brain. You can measure that pretty easily with a monitor these days. Get more and more blood pumping into your brain cells and see what happens. More oxygen. Endorphins get released.

"And even if you can't do five miles, just increase aerobic exercise each day. Feel the results!

"Sedentary lifestyles lead to wheelchairs and early senility. It's not hard to figure out. The studies really aren't rocket science. Check out the difference between those who make exercise a daily endeavor when they're in their eighties versus those trapped in wheelchairs in nursing homes."

"Is this why people around Hope seem to live so long? Some of the people here must be over 100 years old and still seem fit and healthy!" said Gus.

"It's true. We all age. The question is how we age. Care for your brain by exercising, even just walking every day, and the difference will be like night to day.

"Kill the couch potato and that increases your cardiovascular fitness. Improve your cardiovascular fitness and you reduce the risk of things like stroke and heart attack.

"And when you exercise more, you get smarter. Your brain doesn't go into dearth and depression in the same way. It comes back when you've lost it, too. It's not gone forever even if you think you've lost it.

"Climb a mountain. Go for a walk. Run. Lift weights. In the winter, cross country ski. Snowshoe. When you exercise hard like that, guess what it does for your sleep?"

"Makes you sleep better."

"Yep! Recreate hard. Rest hard. Activity's not only part of fueling your brain, but so is intentional inactivity. Of course, rest and solitude are also key to FUELING Your Brain, too."

Fuel Your Brain with Restful Practices

"You fuel your brain through what you're eating, exercising, and when you get regular and consistent rest," Mr. Turnquest continued.

"Good rest isn't something we leave to chance if you want to live in Hope. It's something we plan for and practice as a habit.

"First, rest in the midst of your day happens when you still yourself. Sit still in a chair and let your muscles relax. Breathe deeply. Silence the chatter going on in your head by dismissing it until later. You might try silently praying prayers of release to God. For example, I will take a break, breath in deeply, then release my breath and say to God, 'Release.' Breathe in deeply. Breathe out, and under your breath say, 'Release.' Others say, 'Take it God' on their exhale.

"Or, if you're holding a grudge against someone, try doing the same thing. Breathe in and think of that person. Then breathe out, saying, 'I Forgive.' Try it, and give your brain a rest and your soul a rest."

Fuel Your Brain With Restful Sleep

"Wow! How do you find the time to do all these things that don't seem like work?" asked Gus.

"Work improves as hope improves. They make our work much more productive and much less stressful. So we actually gain more productive time.

"Gus, it's really hard to keep hope alive when you're fatigued and tired. Our brains crave regular sleep and simply malfunction when we don't get good sleep.

"Not only does lack of sleep lead to mental impairment. Lack of sleep leads to emotional impairment."

"I see that in my kids," Gus interjected. "They get whiny and moody when they don't get their sleep. I think I just don't pay as much attention to it in myself."

"Yeah, adolescents are especially sleep-deprived in most places! Most of them! And it leads to all kind of mistakes, moodiness, and an inability to do schoolwork."

"Yeah," Gus agreed. "When I was a teenager, a few of us did an experiment to see how long we could stay up. I think we almost missed two nights of sleep."

"How did it work for you?"

"Gotta say I pretty much hated my life and everyone else's life! I almost got into a car accident on night two. Pretty stupid!"

"It's crazy. Lack of sleep leads to all kinds of traffic accidents, mistakes, and much lower performance on student tests. So why wouldn't you think that lack of sleep would affect ability to hope as well?

"If you want to live into your purpose and your potential, you've got to obey the laws of restful sleep. It's one of the key strategies of self-leadership in Hope.

"Sleep restores you, and if you don't get enough sleep consistently, you're just not going to think as well. And when you don't think as well, you're going to stop living as well. Your hope goes away.

"In Hope, we do something pretty radical when it comes to sleep. We turn off electronics, dim the lights, maybe light candles, and let the rhythm of darkness help our bodies start to rest when the sun goes down.

"Maybe we sit around a fire or a fireplace, but often, it's more relaxing conversation. Maybe reading a book. Sipping on some herbal tea. Nothing with caffeine for sure!

"Then I also practice something that keeps all fear at bay each night. When I get in bed, the first thing I do is rehearse what I'm grateful for. It's almost like magic! It calms my mind and I breathe easily."

"Similar to how you start your day, right?" said Gus.

"Yes, try listing what you're grateful for by either saying it to yourself or putting it on paper. You'll actually feel your brain start to rest."

"I don't have a problem going to sleep," said Gus. "But I sometimes wake up in the middle of the night and can't get back to sleep. I start thinking about things. Usually, it's things I need to do. Problems to solve."

"Is that working for you, Gus?"

"No! I'd much rather be asleep. I think it's likely me allowing the fears to take control."

"Exactly," said Turnquest. "Which one of us really brings our brilliant self to work at 2:00 a.m.? Would you want a self-leadership way to approach waking up in the middle of the night that will actually help?"

"Totally! I see that middle of the night stuff as a curse!"

"Here's what I do. When I wake up and issues start running through my mind, I ask God to help me remember to address those things in the day. Or I write them down on a paper near my bed. Then I remind God of something He said in the Bible, and I ask Him to enable me to go back to sleep."

"What's in the Bible about sleep?" asked Gus.

"Well, it says that too much sleep isn't wise, but that living well leads to restful sleep. In Proverbs 3:24, it says when you learn how to live wisely then, *'When you lie down, you will not be afraid; when you lie down, your sleep will be sweet.'* That's a pretty significant benefit of wise living, isn't it?"

"I won't argue with that," said Gus.

"It says in Psalm 127, *'It's in vain you rise up early and stay up late, toiling for food to eat—God grants sleep to those he loves.'*

"In other words, worry and late nights aren't going to fuel your dreams, and definitely not your body! But God grants sleep to those He loves. God is the one who actually gives you sleep.

"So just remind God, 'God, you love me. I can't control all that's got to be done. You can. But you love me!'"

"So you think I should try that, huh?"

"What's to lose? Do it and watch what happens. Call me crazy, but it works! Next thing I know, the sunlight's coming in the window and it's morning. A good night's sleep is worth its weight in gold!"

"I'll try that approach," replied Gus.

"Sleep as a habit used to be ignored like you'd ignore a car you parked in the driveway for the night. And you pay the price! You know what happens when you're chronically sleep-deprived! You're moody. You eat junk. You get easily angered and agitated. You don't need a Ph.D. to figure out that's not good, right?

"But fuel your brain with good sleep and it improves your memory, curbs inflammation, improves your creativity, and sharpens your ability to pay attention.

"Pay attention to your sleep patterns. Go to bed at roughly the same time each night. Read or relax before bed. Don't watch television or do work

"You can have incredible intelligence and education. But fail to fuel your brain with sleep and forget it. It's even been said that those who practice positive sleep habits live longer!

"There's no medal for not listening to your brain and failing to do what's in its best interest. Some people do best when they take a short nap in the middle of the day; we encourage it around here! Some of our shops close for an hour or two, like they do in Mexico."

Fuel Your Brain with Food

"So fuel your brain with exercise and sleep then," said Gus. "Is that it?"

"Well, one more. Third key to the FUELING Your Brain Habit: fuel your body with the right food to create the best energy. Discouragement and depression can be triggered or exacerbated by food habits that quickly increase the levels of glucose in our blood, then trigger our need to produce insulin to counteract it. We get a shot of energy, soon followed by a lull and a fatigue.

"Our brains feel the fatigue and they interpret it as, 'I'm tired. This is bad. My life is bad.'

"Fuel your brain with good, lean proteins, with fresh vegetables, healthy fruits, and with a smaller amount of grains, and you start to realize you're not getting the swings of ups and downs. You don't feel groggy or cranky as much. Things just seem better. And they are!

"When you've got more consistent energy, you feel more productive and you get things done. You're not counting on coffee or other stimulants to get you through.

"I realize this isn't rocket science. You don't need a master's degree in nutrition to understand this. But practicing it—that's where the rubber meets the road!

"FUELING your brain makes a huge difference!

"Are you ready now to hear the other physical thing that makes a huge difference in Hope?" Mr. Turnquest asked.

"Sure!" said Gus. "What's that?"

Habit of Hope:
Fueling Your Brain

Summarized: Maintain and grow the health and wellbeing of your brain as a regular priority. Your brain's physical health is key to your hope and fulfilling your bigger purpose. Fuel your brain with regular movement, restful practices, and peaceful sleep. Eat food that enables your brain to work at maximum capacity.

Realized: What benefit or benefits might you (and/or others) see or experience by you practicing the habit of *Fueling Your Brain* as a way of life?

Evaluated: How far along are you in the habit of *Fueling Your Brain* presently? (1 not at all to 10 completely)

1   2   3   4   5   6   7   8   9   10

Applied: What will you do to practice or grow this habit of *Fueling Your Brain*?

Habit Releaser:

Find a time during your day just to sit still and proactively relax, breathe, and release your anxiety or toxic thoughts inhabiting your brain.

Turn off electronics and dim lights an hour before going to bed. Experience the peace and serenity of your own surroundings.

Increase protein and vegetables and limit sweets each day. Start your day with eggs, protein drinks, and eliminate high sugar or high carbs for breakfast. Notice your energy and brain functioning when you do.

CHAPTER 23

HYDRATING: HYDRATING CONTINUALLY

"If there is magic on this planet, it is contained in water."

— Loran Eisley

The two men walked up toward Lake Hope and Gus picked a flat rock to skip across the water, ricocheting across multiple waves.

"That, right there's, the next Habit of Hope," said Mr. Turnquest.

"Skipping rocks?" said Gus, half-joking but also half-serious.

"No. Water. A lot of it. HYDRATING Continually," answered Mr. Turnquest.

"Hope and hydration are linked, but many don't make the connection," Mr. Turnquest said.

"Your healthy body is gonna be filled with water—and watered constantly. In general, men should have a total body water percentage between 50 and 65 percent, while the ideal range for women is between 45 and 60 percent. But more is better than less."

"And that's connected to Hope?" asked Gus.

"It's the habit of restoring the water in your body to healthy levels. Personally, I used to start my day with a couple of cups of coffee. Then pretty much just have a sip or two from a water fountain during the day. Maybe a Coke during lunch. But that's about it!

"Do you get it? My body was basically drained of H^2O. My heart had to work overtime. And how do you think this affected my brain?

"Your body depends on water, not just to survive, but to thrive! Every single cell, tissue, and organ uses water for everything from lubrication to waste removal. Each day you lose water every time you use the bathroom, sweat, or just breathe. And when it gets hot out, you know you're losing it much quicker.

"I realize this may not bode well for your vision of just how smart your friend Mr. T is, but for years, I had a dry mouth, headaches, fatigue, felt lightheaded, and had dark urine. And I thought the situation was hopeless! You'd think I would have made a connection! I needed to drink more water. A lot more water!" Mr. Turnquest said.

The Message from Randy Whitaker

"I finally made the connection by watching my friend Randy Whitaker. Randy was continually sipping from a water bottle. Constantly! One day I told him I was feeling dizzy and kind of tired.

"Randy asked whether I was drinking enough water.

"My response: I laughed out loud. 'I don't know, Randy. Are you?'

"'Rodney,' he said, 'why wouldn't I? My body runs on water!'

"'How much water do you drink?' I asked Randy.

"'Eight-eight!' he said.

"'What's eight-eight?' I asked.

"'At least eight, eight-ounce glasses of water every day. At least that!' he said. Some health gurus teach you should drink half your body weight in ounces. So if you weigh 160 pounds, drink eighty ounces of water per day.

"'I drink one as soon as I get up. After all, my body's been dehydrating all night long. So I start my day with a big glass of water. Then every time I pee, I replace what I lost. If I drink a cup of coffee, I follow it with a water chaser.

"'Coffee's not a hydrator, Rodney. Do you ever notice that the more coffee you drink, the more you go to the bathroom? Then whenever I notice my urine isn't clear, I drink a glass of water.

"'And if you don't like water so much,' Randy said, 'then drink fruit juices, vegetable juices, or herbal teas. When you can start your day with a big glass of some green juice, even better!

"'And yes, avoid the sugar water! You don't need that messing with your sugar levels.

"'Rodney, I even learned that I feel my best when I get water from fruits and vegetables, like watermelon, tomatoes, or apples. Cucumbers. Strawberries. Things with water in them taste great!'"

"Gus, Randy was a lifesaver! He was absolutely right! And within days after focusing on hydration, everything in my body and my mind started feeling and working better.

"Hydration's now a vital habit of Hope!" Mr. Turnquest concluded.

Remembering to Hydrate

"So how do you remember to keep doing that?" asked Gus.

"Just keep a water bottle with you wherever you go. If you don't want to buy those expensive, fancy bottles, just keep any clean bottle with a screw top cap with you. Refill it from the tap.

"Sometimes, I even add a slice of lemon or lime to mine just to give it a little taste. Or if you get bored with just water, try coconut water. At every meal, have at least one tall glass of water. Definitely drink a glass before and after exercising!

"Now I even pay attention to the color of my pee. 'Light yellow. Be mellow. Dark yellow. Get a drink, fellow!'

Gus laughed out loud. "Quite the poet, aren't you?"

"Most people totally underestimate how much water they need to be at their hope-filled and physical best. If the human brain is composed of 95 percent water, blood is 82 percent water, and your lungs are 90 percent water, what do you think happens when you don't replace that water? I'm pretty adamant about this now! Water's critical to having a balance in your body's systems and in avoiding the stress that affects you constantly when you're dehydrated.

"If it's the case that a 2 percent drop in body water can cause a small shrinkage in the brain, impair your muscular coordination, and decrease your ability to concentrate, why wouldn't teachers be shouting this message to their students from the rooftop?"

"This makes so much sense, Mr. T," said Gus nodding. "I'm surprised this message even has to be taught and adopted as a habit. But what would help us keep this on our minds throughout the day?"

"You do want you heart to work smoothly, right? Do it for your heart! Just staying hydrated will keep your heart from having to work so hard. Your blood will simply flow through your veins more freely.

"Do it for your skin! HYDRATING is also important for your skin! There's not much that drinking more water won't help when it comes to your overall health, Gus. It's a no-brainer! It's just not something you'll see a whole lot of advertising about!

"Of course, your body affects your ability to stay living in hope! Here's what will happen. Become a hydrator and watch how other things become easier for you. I even believe that keeping a healthy weight is much easier when you're plenty hydrated.

"That's a lot of benefits for something that doesn't cost much!" said Gus.

"Agreed," said Mr. Turnquest. "So many of the best things we can do for ourselves don't cost much. And if it's easier for your body to lower stress levels, how might that affect your mind and your soul?"

"I totally think this is right on. It's so simple, it's genius," said Gus. "So besides toting around a bottle of water, how can I remember to drink from it—to turn this into a real habit of hope?"

"Just start by keeping a checklist. Do it on your phone if that's easy for you. Just put a list from one to eight. Then do it for thirty days. See what happens. My guess is you'll become much more aware for the rest of your life. I think you'll live longer, too!"

And with that, Mr. Turnquest picked up and handed Gus a bottle of water—then picked up one for himself.

"Here's to your hydrated health, Gus! Inside and out!"

Habit of Hope:
Hydrating Continually

Summarized: Hydrate your body with water continually and watch how other things become easier for you. Drink water as soon as you get up each morning and regularly throughout the day.

Realized: What benefit or benefits might you (and/or others) see or experience by you practicing the habit of *Hydrating Continually* as a way of life?

Evaluated: How far along are you in the habit of *Hydrating Continually* presently? (1 not at all to 10 completely)

1   2   3   4   5   6   7   8   9   10

Applied: What will you do to practice or grow the habit of *Hydrating Continually*?

Habit Releaser:

Try drinking your body weight in ounces each day to get used to how much water your body requires to be fully hydrated.

Keep a water bottle with you throughout the day and sip water regularly as a habit of hydrating.

Each time you urinate or drink a cup of coffee, drink at least an eight ounce glass of water.

CHAPTER 24

OVERCOMING:
OVERCOMING SETBACKS

"The only person you are destined to
become is the person you decide to be."

— Ralph Waldo Emerson

That afternoon, Gus and Mr. Turnquest continued their walk by heading over to the Kunjamuk River. This shallow, reed-filled river is ideal for those who would want to paddle and unwind their souls among lily pads, cattails, meandering bends, marshes, open areas, and beaver dams.

Though the name Kunjamuk seems to come from an Indian or French word, others believe that long ago, someone might have stepped out of his birch bark canoe into a pile of muck on the bank, thus giving it its name.

As the two walked along its banks, Mr. Turnquest began to share some history others may not think about when they witness the beauty of the Kunjamuk.

"It's a nice place now, but at one point, the Kunjamuk and rivers like it were the key to the Adirondacks' economy. The Great Sacandaga River was another one. It was what brought work to the region. Wood. Logging. The timber here has been harvested for more than a century," Mr. Turnquest said. "An early story of the Adirondacks was about finding creative ways to bust log jams.

"Before trucking became the means to transport felled logs to the sawmills, trees would be cut in the fall and moved to the rivers during the winter. Work was tough! Larger trees needed to be put on skids, wrapped in chains, and pulled through the snow on horses or oxen. Smaller trees could be loaded by pulleys or chains on wooden sleds. Then when spring came and the rivers were running high, the logs would be pushed in and floated toward the mills."

"That stuff interests you, I see," said Gus.

"Gus, all of life illustrates God's truth. The question is: Will we take time to see it?

"You know one key principle I see when I see the Kunjamuk?"

"What's that?"

"Undoing log jams. OVERCOMING setbacks."

"Log jams?" Gus questioned.

"Yeah. In log driving, floating logs to the mill, some unforeseen rock would catch a log and before long, hundreds of logs would pile up in gigantic jams. From bank to bank, the river would be piled with logs.

"Why am I telling you this? Because those loggers knew that log jams were to be expected! They prepared themselves with sticks of dynamite, long pikes to jostle the logs, and even special logging boats known as jam boats. Usually, it took three men just to maneuver these flat bottom boats to unclog the tangled messes of logs. It was dangerous work. Lives were lost when someone would slip between a log and fall into the freezing river.

"But you have to believe that those men would celebrate wildly when the log jams were opened, and the Adirondacks' rivers were once again turned into moving streams of progress.

Expect Adversity...Don't Be Surprised by It

"Here in Hope, we expect adversity like a logger expects a log jam! We're not surprised that things take time. We're ready to tackle setbacks in health, in business, in relationships."

"And I'm assuming this relates to another Habit of Hope, doesn't it?" asked Gus.

"Yep! And the next Habit of Hope involves OVERCOMING SETBACKS by seeing them, not as an adversary, but as an advantage. It's the storms that help trees develop deeper roots.

"Can you see it that way?"

"Mr. T, theoretically, that makes sense. My setbacks have been more the inside stuff. My own anger and disappointment. My hatred for my job. And, of course, my marriage problems!"

"Well, Winston Churchill once said, 'If you're going through hell, keep going!' What if…just what if…your adversity is actually a clue to your purpose? What if the things that most seem to keep you back, if unlocked, could catapult you to joy and even break loose a path down the river for you and others?

"I realize sometimes we think that whenever we set out to do something, especially something good or meaningful, the world will just cooperate with us. People will cheer and not jeer. Buyers will open their wallets and willingly pay our prices. Even God will make the way clear and line up all the situations to our advantage.

"It's not the way we would devise things if we ran the world, I get that. But some things are true, even if you don't believe them. And the truth is that adversity is a pathway toward hope. But we still have a choice to let it win or to fight it," Mr. Turnquest said.

"Yeah, Mr. T, I've especially thought that my own family would collaborate and certainly not criticize. That's the hardest adversity, because it cuts so deeply, if you know what I mean. You'd think, 'If she's not for me, is there something wrong with me? Am I flawed?'"

Don't Take Adversity Personally

"It's hard not to take adversity personally," Mr. Turnquest agreed. "But often it's actually the means to a better end, even if in the moment, adversity seems like your enemy. Gus, there is an enemy that wants to steal, kill, and destroy you and your destiny—keep you from discovering and engaging your bigger purpose. The Resistance. And the Resistance may use adversity against you. But you can't let it! You've got to fight to see adversity as part of your advantage! What stands in your way can *become* your way. Your struggle can make you stronger and more resilient.

"So often we get it in our heads that when we don't win, we lose. Or we see ourselves as losers. But life doesn't work that way. Stuff happens. Pipes burst. Sales go to the competition. Relationships break down. The key to staying in hope is what we do next. Do we see it as a loss? Or a simple setback to be overcome?"

Gus picked up a log and heaved it into the river, as he listened, realizing so much of his life had been infiltrated by setbacks, logs, and logjams.

"Why did God allow so many logjams to come my way?" asked Gus, in distress even as he said the words.

"I can't speak for God about your life specifically. I know you've been through pain, and I'm so, so sorry for that pain. But I can say that each time you persevere despite the odds, you build your storehouse of hope-filled resilience. It's just the way things work. You work out hard, you break down the muscle, and the muscle become stronger.

Choosing to Win and Learn and Pay Attention

"The thing is, Gus, it's not really whether you win or lose; it's whether you win and learn. You've got to be okay that with many things, there's just no shortcut. Win and learn. Come to a dead end, look for another path. No shortcut."

"I hear you, Mr. T. Maybe it's like the story you mentioned of the boy who's thinking he's helping the butterfly by working with it to get out of the cocoon once it starts to struggle. It doesn't seem to be making much progress. He grabs scissors and cuts the cocoon away and frees it. But instead of flying, its wings stay stuck, gooey, and its body swollen. It wasn't able to fly and soon died."

"And the lesson there?"

"The lesson—the butterfly needed to struggle to become what it was supposed to be. The boy learned that the struggle was part of the process of growth, what ultimately allowed it to fly."

"Yes! You get it, Gus! And it's that adversity that gives you a clue to your ability to fulfill your purpose. Very few people actually take the time to study their own adversity. Sadly, it's the unusual person who actually takes the time to listen to his or her own life and see the threads of deeper meaning."

"What would that look like, Mr. T?"

"It looks like paying attention to the answers to some questions. Clues to your purpose."

"What kinds of questions?" Gus asked.

"Well, if you believe there are no accidents in life, then even your adversities are no accident. I realize some of the rougher events become super-challenging to see this way. But one of the best exercises I ever did involved a journal and a few key questions."

"What were the questions? I'd be open to giving it a shot," Gus said.

"First: What were the toughest seasons or experiences of your life?

"Second: If you were to learn something really valuable from these seasons or experiences, what would you learn?

"Third: What expertise would you have to offer others based on what you experienced?"

Expertise from Tough Experience

"Wow!" said Gus with a look of understanding. "I could see I might be an expert in helping hopeless people find hope based on what you just said! Hope in life. Hope in career issues. Maybe even hope in struggling marriages!"

"That was pretty quick, Gus! Sometimes, just a few key questions can bring understanding that seemed hidden forever! It really doesn't need to take that long."

"I think you've known it for a while, Mr. T!"

"Well, I've wondered whether that valley of dry bones dream I had about you, and the fact that you actually came to Hope, had something to do with it. Somehow your real dreams couldn't be realized until you caught a picture of what hope could look like— look like for you. You needed a vision of what was possible. You needed a glimpse of Hope."

"I needed it desperately. I didn't even realize how much I needed it" exclaimed Gus.

"When it comes to living in hope, your perspective is your choice. You can either see yesterday and today's challenge as a means to a bigger end or as nothing more than a challenge. You choose what you focus on and what you look for. God won't take that choice away. In fact, God can use that to build your faith and make your peace and joy deeper if you want it to. It's up to you, isn't it?

"I've known enough people who are literally in prison to know that how they see overcoming setbacks is the key to good attitudes or defeat. They can allow the bars in their surroundings to crush them or to build them.

"It was Victor Frankl, a survivor of a brutal German concentration camp who wrote, *'Everything can be taken from a man but one thing: the last of the human freedoms—to choose one's attitude in any given set of circumstances, to choose one's own way.'*

"That man was resilient, wasn't he? Frankl realized that having a bigger purpose could enable someone to get through the most difficult time. I've read that book. Think I need to reread it."

"Whenever you need to! And resilience is a great word for it! Resilience grows when you're imprisoned by challenges and setbacks, you get one free choice: to make the choice to hope, or not hope. Faith grows there too. As Andy Dufresne says in the movie, *Shawshank Redemption*, *"Hope is a good thing, maybe the best of things, and no good thing ever dies."*

"I love that movie," said Gus, as he nodded in agreement.

"And who hasn't felt trapped under miles of rock, no light seeping through?" said Mr. Turnquest with a knowing look. "I've felt that way. Especially when I lost Alice to breast cancer. In her final months, we still had some laughs together. But I knew those would be some of our last. When she passed, at first, I was crushed. For a while I had thought God would heal her. I really did!"

"I can't imagine, Mr. T. I'm so sorry for your loss."

"None of us gets to fully escape tough times. Hope or no hope. No matter how strong or powerful or confident you are, tough times come your way. And they're gonna do what they can to cause you to crumble and snap. Even if you feel strong and mighty one day, you'll feel scared the next."

"I'm sorry I didn't even know she died."

"Yeah, thank you. It was hard. I won't hide that. Stuff's gonna happen and fear's gonna knock at your door, Habits of Hope or not. But when they do, the OVERCOMING SETBACKS habit, by God's power, will make all the difference. It's the light of truth that pushes back darkness. I don't say this to cause fear; I say it because it's the truth. The hardest part of tough times is hanging on to hope. And that's the part that's gonna shape you as well."

"Yeah, I don't think I've allowed it to shape me for the better, unfortunately, Mr. Turnquest. I think I've spent a lot of time getting bitter instead of better. This habit's gonna make a big difference for me."

"It's all about what you see my friend. Do you see a ditch or a future foundation for a building? Do you see a storm or a way to water the grass? Do you see your past as a curse or as what created the strength and wisdom you have today? My sense is that you're about to see this log jam break open in ways you never could have imagined. When this thing starts flowing, it's gonna flow so quickly and with so much momentum no one would be crazy enough to get in its way.

"OVERCOMING setbacks will set you free. Now is your time to overcome adversity and achieve your bigger purpose!"

Habit of Hope:

Overcoming Setbacks

Summarized: Since adversity is part of life, choose to grow and persevere and even gain experience and expertise through it. Overcoming your setbacks is your personal courageous choice. Expect adversity and counter it with resilience, faith, and hope to overcome your setbacks and continue living into your bigger purpose.

Realized: What benefit or benefits might you (and/or others) see or experience by you practicing the *overcoming setbacks habit* as a way of life?

Evaluated: How far along are you in the *overcoming setbacks habit* presently? (1 not at all to 10 completely)

1   2   3   4   5   6   7   8   9   10

Applied: What will you do to practice or grow the *overcoming setbacks habit*?

Habit Releaser:

Answer these three key questions in a journal or with a group:

1. What were the toughest seasons or experiences of your life?

2. If you were to learn something really valuable from these seasons or experiences, what would you learn?

3. What expertise would you have to offer others based on what you experienced?"

CHAPTER 25

PROGRESSING:
PROGRESSING TOWARD YOUR VISION OR DREAM

"Without continual growth and progress, such words as improvement, achievement, and success have no meaning."

— Benjamin Franklin

A s the two continued their walk, Turnquest stopped, looked Gus in the eye, and said, "I know you've already heard a lot, but the Habit of Hope I'd like to introduce you to now can't be left out."

"I'm in!" said Gus. "Go for it!"

"I wouldn't be surprised if you've heard this before because it's a wise old saying from a Vietnam era U.S. military commander by the name of Creighton Abrams, Jr."

"Try me," said Gus.

"Abrams said, 'When eating an elephant, take one bite at a time.'

"If you're like me, you're not a big fan of good intentions. Nor are you a fan of people with pipe dreams they never act on. I think that's why so many people shrink back from people with dreams. They've seen too many people who talk a good game, but in the end do nothing."

"That drives Amy crazy. She hates when I have big dreams of buying a new house, fixing up our house, or even starting a new company."

"And why does that drive her crazy?"

"Because I am pretty much all talk, no do."

"And did she have a point?"

"Maybe."

The Progressing Habit

"Gus, that's why one of the most valuable Habits of Hope is called 'Progressing.' Progressing Toward Your Vision Daily. It's the habit of taking a single bite out of your elephant. It's doing simple, doable things each day to move toward the bigger vision of what you most want."

"Yeah, I'm not a fan of good intentions," Gus said. "I've had enough of them in my life. I've wanted to change things in my marriage. Doesn't happen. I've wanted to move toward a fulfilling career. Doesn't happen."

"It's the little things, right?" agreed Turnquest.

"Frankly, I'm tired of my own good intentions," Gus confessed with anger in his voice. "So I guess you could say I've lacked hope that I could ever change me! I know this time with you is changing that, but I'm actually fearful that once I leave Hope, I won't be able to follow through and live these Habits of Hope."

"I understand, Gus. And you're not alone. It's the same thing that causes people to get fed up with New Year's resolutions. Most certainly don't have a life plan.... Most plan for things like education or finances, but fail to plan a life.

"Would you want that to change?"

"Of course I would!" Gus exclaimed. "But when does it make sense to give up trying when even our own intentions feel unreasonable? It's kind of like hearing someone say, 'It's the thought that counts.' No. Not really. Good intentions and good thoughts don't do much."

"Unless," Mr. Turnquest said, then paused.

"Unless what?"

"Unless you create the Habit of PROGRESSING as part of your daily life intentionally, then other things, including other people's agendas, won't squeeze you out."

The Good Intentions Equation

"You see, you're right about frustration. I'd say that equation of Frustration = Good Intentions + No Action. Desire with no activity. It feels ridiculous, and you say what I used to tell myself,

'I can't change! Things will never change!' That's gets old, and then you lose hope, right?"

"I'm tracking," said Gus.

"*But* there's another side of the equation. Action without good intentions = Futility. When you just do things with no plan, vision, or bigger desire, then you're just doing stuff with no direction. And then people still most wonder, 'Why does my life lack meaning?' or 'Why don't I have any real purpose!'

"In the book of Proverbs, it says '*When there is no vision, people perish.*' You get that, right? Without any bigger hope to make things better, people don't thrive. They cast off any real discipline or activity. Like a stinky vegetable, they grow stale and rot."

Clear Vision and 90-Day Objectives

"The Habit of PROGRESSING starts with a clear vision of your desired future. Or even better, getting clarity on the future God has in store for you," Turnquest explained.

"Is there some practice to help you do that?" questioned Gus.

"At the beginning of every quarter, I personally spend a morning or so envisioning what I want to exist in ninety days that doesn't exist now. I call these my 'ninety-day objectives.'

"And what kinds of things do those include for you?"

"They include things like 'I've finished restoring my car.' 'I've created the plan for my new business venture.' 'I weigh what I did when I married Alice.' You see, plans are doable and achievable when they're toward a clear vision. They free us to make progress and focus on a few important things at a time.

"I used to think God was anti-plan. Just faith. Then I read a prayer in the book of Psalms that basically says God loves our plans! *'May he give you the desire of your heart and make all your plans succeed.'* It's Psalm 20:4.

"I tell you! If more business leaders, government leaders, any leaders, would just get this! God is pro-vision and pro-plan! He wants us to dream big dreams and have a vision for progress. But then God wants our plans to succeed, not lay in some drawer or in a pile."

Gus stood motionless for a few seconds, taking in what he'd just heard.

"I get that, and I also get the frustration of having desires and even plans, but not making progress."

"And that's why you've got to dream big and act small. Have a vision, then progress toward it each day. Then pray like crazy, of course!

"I've got huge dreams, Gus! I dream of seeing what's happening in Hope spread to every town and nation in the world. And right now, I'm taking action on that."

"What do you mean?" Gus asked.

"I'm sharing this idea with someone who has the gifts to take the vision to a crazy number of people."

"Me?"

"Yeah, you!" Mr. Turnquest exclaimed. "I see my mission involving just one person at a time. For me, it's about going deep and letting wide happen over time. That's the power of mentoring. Of coaching. Of living this idea. And I've got an incredible role model."

"Who's that?" Gus asked.

"His name was Jesus. Heard of him?"

"Ha! Yeah, I've heard of him!"

"Jesus lived one day at a time moving toward a supernatural vision of establishing the Kingdom of God. He said we should pray for God's will to be done 'on earth as it is in heaven.' Jesus went with the 'go big by going small' strategy. He entrusted His Kingdom message and lifestyle to a small group of followers with the idea that they would live it and share it with others."

Start With One Small Step

"It's so easy to try to do everything and end up doing nothing. That's why you've got to know your vision, then do the one thing you can each day to move in that direction with a tangible action step. Have a big dream. Then act small. Have a big mindset. Then have a small mindset. Just 'one thing.'"

"What do you mean by 'one thing'? How do you know what that 'one thing' is?"

"Well, for some, it changes every day. And because you can't do everything, you'll want to pray and seek wisdom to know your 'one thing' for that day. And it will take discernment to discover it. It's often something that's important, but not urgent. My guess is no one's gonna be breathing down your neck to do it. But if you do it today, then do the 'one thing' tomorrow…. Things compound over time. It's putting your money in a good interest-bearing account and seeing the compound effect take place. It starts off slow and seemingly unimpressive. But then momentum takes over, and before long, things multiply.

"I think many of us tend to overestimate what we can do in a year, but underestimate what we can do in three years or three decades. What I'm saying is staying committed to one thing over time brings about results."

Focusing Questions to Start Each Day

"How does that work in everyday life? Knowing your one thing, that is?"

"So here's a simple group of questions I start with every day just so I stay on track with making progress each day," Mr. Turnquest replied. "Just write these down and answer them:

1. What's important about today?

2. What must be done today?

3. What's important for the future?"

"Wow! Great questions! I'm gonna write those down."

"Good idea. When you get clarity on these, you're allowing your bigger vision, and even your values, to influence what you do daily. Then you don't get flustered, and you accomplish what matters most—the stuff that's not urgent, but important and enduring. Just one day at a time."

"You do this daily, huh?"

"I do, but do that if it serves you. There's no requirement to ask them every day. Try doing it for a while, and see how it works. But when you find yourself feeling overwhelmed, start your day with these. So on days when you've got someone in town or a project due, don't get panicked that you're not doing other things. Just ask, 'What's important about today?' Sometimes, you'll find your family time, or even the care of your own soul, trumps business or work. But that's okay. At least you've been intentional about it."

"Bet you feel a lot of peace when you do that, don't you?" Gus said.

"Exactly! A lot of peace! Over time, you practice the Habit of PROGRESSING, and your influence and income increase exponentially. And you're a lot nicer to be around because you're making progress in what matters to you. If you want to have ongoing joy and fulfillment, the secret is just one word—progress. Make just a little progress each day.

"One of my mentors once told me, 'Life's not a sprint. It's a marathon.' The urge either to try to do it all at once, or at the other extreme, just quit, can strike at any time. Fight that! PROGRESSING. One thing. One step.

"It takes tenacity. I'm not saying it's simple or easy. It can be very difficult, at least at first. But start practicing PROGRESSING and become better and better at doing the next 'one thing.' Then, Gus, you'll lead nations!

292

"But just take one bite of the elephant for now. You'll see!" Mr. Turnquest promised.

Habit of Hope:

Progressing Toward Your Vision or Dream

Summarized: Gain clarity of your vision and take small steps regularly to move in that direction each day. Don't worry about doing too much at once. Instead, ask yourself regular questions to gain clarity on what's most important and must be done each day to move a little bit farther in the right direction.

Realized: What benefit or benefits might you (and/or others) see or experience by you practicing the *Progressing Toward Your Vision or Dream Habit* as a way of life?

Evaluated: How far along are you in the *Progressing Toward Your Vision or Dream Habit* presently? (1 not at all to 10 completely)

1   2   3   4   5   6   7   8   9   10

Applied: What will you do to practice or grow the *Progressing Toward Your Vision or Dream Habit*?

Habit Releaser:

On a piece of paper or a journal, write out, then answer the three focusing questions each day for at least one week. See what happens! Note your progress.

    1. What's important about today?

    2. What must be done today?

    3. What's important for the future?"

CHAPTER 26

EMPOWERING: EMPOWERING OTHERS TO HOPE

"As we look ahead into the next century, leaders
will be those who empower others."

— Bill Gates

"**M**r. T, these habits all fill me with hope that real change is possible." said Gus. "I feel like the last few days of both experiencing Hope and learning these habits gives me new vision. But even if I do make real progress, how do I keep from slipping back? I don't want to be the old me. I want to remain in Hope!"

"The absolute best way," answered Mr. Turnquest, "to remain in hope for a lifetime is by becoming a spreader of the message—

actively fostering the habits of hope in others. Inspired people inspire people. It's kind of how the cycle of life works.

"Napoleon Bonaparte once said, *A leader is a dealer in hope.*'

"Leaders help others see something that may not at first be obvious. Hope is like that! Once you know *and* live the Habits of Hope, the best thing you can do is to help others come to hope. In fact, helping others to discover and engage hope may actually be the best way to help yourself. It's both incredibly generous and incredibly selfish!"

"Yeah, I agree with the saying 'Most people live lives of quiet desperation,'" said Gus. I've been around enough teenagers to see them hiding in self-hatred, or even going to the point of hurting their own bodies. I've seen moms locked up and trapped with their own kids. I have friends who hate their jobs and feel stuck and hopeless. And I've known older people, the ones supposedly in their golden years, saying they think the best years of their lives are already behind them."

"Gus, I know we'd all like to just offer a pill to people that will bring them hope and happiness. But it's not that way. Sure, medication may be the absolute right, temporary option to get out of a deep, deep hole that's affected your body chemistry. But it should not be a long-term solution, that's for sure!"

"So, do you see chronic anxiety and depression as physical?"

"They affect the physical and are physical problems for sure. But often the roots of anxiety and depression are spiritual. They require spiritual solutions—or at least that's a key part of the solution. That's why a good number of the Habits of Hope involve a spiritual dimension. The spiritual affects the physical and vice versa. And they all affect the emotional."

"I realize that's why we need these habits Mr. T!"

"I also think that far too many people feel totally alone or helpless about overcoming the mess in their thinking. It's like hopelessness invades your soul and you have nowhere to turn. People need to know this message of *hope*. Others need to hear this practical message of a better way of life! It burns me up that so many out there feel like I've been feeling for so long. I feel their pain and it stinks. It really stinks!"

Mr. Turnquest looked at Gus and was shocked by what he saw. Tears were streaming down Gus' face. They were dripping off his cheek in a regular cadence.

"What's going on Gus?"

"I don't know." Gus paused and wiped his tears with his shirtsleeve. "I think it just hit me—all the people in my life whose lives could be vastly different if they knew what I now know and did something with these! I want others to know how God offers them tangible ways to experience hope and purpose, then sustain it.

"I've been an absolute idiot to Amy. I think she's probably been more patient with me than I deserved. She needs to know this stuff. I want her to know there's really a way to infuse hope into our lives. Hearing she's blessed. Appreciating the good. Believing God is at work. And together investing in our dreams. If you could speak to her and share all this, that would breathe life into her—instead of the crap I've been feeding her!

"If only I'd known what you've shared with me early in our marriage, we wouldn't be in this hole! If only I'd lived this way and been an example of a hope-filled dad to my kids instead of a demanding, selfish, stubborn—jerk!"

"I love your heart," Mr. Turnquest said.

"You think I've got a heart!" said Gus, half-kidding.

"Ha! Yeah, Partner, I *know* you have a heart! It's the heart I saw in you as a kid. It's never gone away. It's why I reached out to you. I know that's the real you, Gus. And I know it's your destiny."

"My kids need to know this! Not the religious stuff I think they've got along the way, but something alive—what I've seen in you and the people in Hope. It's this Hope and this way of being intentional about your life you practice that seems to transform people. I don't know if my kids have ever experienced anything like that!

"So what would it look like if my heart came back to life?" Gus asked.

Bringing Hope to Others

"You're already seeing it! When your heart's alive, you start thinking about others. You start caring that others find what you've found. You hope for others, not just yourself! And it starts with those close to you. You want that for your family. Your friends. You want that for your kids."

"And I realize that when it's 'all about me,' it says my heart's pretty dead. And from all I've shared with you, I think you can tell my hearts been basically flatlined. All about me! And I'm ready for a change," Gus shared, as again, tears came to his eyes.

"The spiritual writer, Frederick Buechner, said something that has stuck with me, '*Whenever you find tears in your eyes, especially unexpected tears, it is well to pay the closest attention.*'"

"And you're thinking I should pay attention, huh?"

"Well, I think you're more surprised than anyone at the tears coming down your face, just because you want others to experience this journey to hope. It was like your soul was telling you something. And it's exactly what the final Habit of Hope is all about."

"What's that?"

"EMPOWERING. Empower Others to Hope. The purpose we've all inherited from the Creator involves the power to bring life and hope to others. It's God's heart coming out of you. It's incredible! That's leadership, Gus. Leadership is helping lead others to hope. The greatest leaders fight to have hope in themselves, then translate that hope to others. Like an alcoholic who's found sobriety, the most powerful thing you can do for someone else, another alcoholic, is sharing your own journey—what you've found. You start by telling your story

The Power of One Person's Story

"One of my favorite stories in the Bible involves the man born blind. Are you familiar with the story?" Mr. Turnquest asked.

"Maybe. But remind me."

"In John 9, there's a story of a guy who was born blind, and Jesus heals him. It's kind of strange how it happens—Jesus spits on the ground, makes mud, glops it on the guy's eyes, then commands him to go wash the mud out in the Pool of Siloam. When he does, he's no longer blind! But then this healed guy gets pummeled by a bunch of skeptics. They question his healing. They question Jesus. They even question the guy's parents.

"The skeptics ask the blind man, 'What did he do to you? We know this man is a sinner!' In desperation, the man born blind tells them, 'Whether he is a sinner or not, I don't know. One thing I do know. I was blind, but now I see.'"

"Wow! I like that," said Gus. "Sure answered them!"

"And that's exactly what's so powerful when you discover hope. You experience the real deal! You were hopeless, but now you're hopeful! It's what happened for me, and it's why I sent you the letter and spent this time with you! I was depressed, stuck, purposeless. But now I'm passionate, free, and excited about my own destiny! And that's what's happening for you right now!

"Until you've fully implemented The Habits of Hope and made a visible change in your life, you definitely don't want to share them with anyone! No one wants to hear more mumbo jumbo that doesn't really work. We do, however, want to know good news."

"Yeah, I had pretty much given up on organized religion," interrupted Gus. "I had started to think the whole thing was bunk, whether Jesus or jihad! And since it hadn't worked for me, why in the world would I tell others?"

"But if it works—*when* it works—then it makes sense to tell others! It would be wrong not to! When you experience authentic Hope, then you'll want to spread the good news. You'll want to share your story. You'll want to talk about each of these Habits with them like I've done for you."

"What would you tell them?"

"Tell them about this way of life and about these Habits. Tell them that God's still at work in the world! Folks don't want to be preached at. I don't. You don't. But we'll listen to someone who's authentic. We'll listen to someone who's got a compelling story. We'll follow someone who's got purpose and someone who knows where they're going!

"We all really want our soul to come alive. I wouldn't know anyone who wouldn't want that!"

"So when you know, and experience these practices bringing your soul to life, then share them. You can't pay enough money for that kind of understanding. No new car, new job, vacation, or even fame and fortune can compare to the value of knowing why you're here and how to fulfill your purpose. Others have no idea this power of purpose and hope is actually available—and their families don't know it. Their communities don't know it. Many churches don't know it. And it may not be their fault! They've simply never encountered credible guides. They don' t know anyone who's experienced a credible journey to Hope!"

Gus looked down in deep thought for what seemed like a long time. Turnquest stood in silence, almost as if recognizing the power of a holy moment.

"Mr. T, first, thank you! I'm overwhelmed with gratitude that you rescued me. Actually, I think you did that literally!" Gus said with a smile.

"I guess I did pull you out of a lake."

"Yeah, you did! But way beyond that, you shared your journey to Hope. But I can't help starting to think of all the people whose lives could be changed by this message—this way of life. I know I'm still just learning, but I want to do for others what you've done for me. Mr. T, God help me, I'd be totally excited to share the Habits with others and share this way of life."

"Gus, the reason the final Habit of Hope is EMPOWERING Others to Hope is because that's not only how the world changes, but it's how we all change. You'll find yourself experiencing purpose as you help others find their purposes. You'll find your hope growing off the charts as you intentionally help others experience transformational hope. That's what life in God's Kingdom looks like. It's one beggar sharing a piece of bread with another beggar."

"When will I know I'm ready to start Empowering Others to Hope?" Gus asked.

"It sure isn't gonna be too long for you! Start practicing the Habits and two things will happen. First, you'll start to see your own spirit come alive. You'll experience happiness again. You'll sense your heart growing, and you'll start to care.

"Second, you'll start seeing others lacking hope all around you. You'll want to share with them the Hope you've found. You'll share your own story.

Sharing Your Way of Life… "Come and See!"

"And Gus, it's not about sharing religion with people. No one wants religion preached at them. But just as Jesus went around teaching people not a new religion, but whole new way of life, you'll be excited to share with others this way of life."

"Is it the same thing?"

"Is what the same thing?"

"The way of life Jesus taught?"

"Well, when Jesus was asked by followers of John the Baptist whether he was God's expected one, or was someone else coming, he told them, as it says in Matthew, '*The blind receive sight, the lame walk, those who have leprosy are cleansed, the deaf hear, the dead are raised, and the good news is proclaimed to the poor.*'

"Do you think these days he would have included the anxious, distraught, and depressed who became full of peace and hope?"

"Totally believe that! When God works in the world, people's lives change radically. The awful diseases of the day get healed. Those impoverished get a message of hope that changes the way they see things. Depression and hopelessness is not only affecting people on a huge scale physically—with an estimated 16 million in the U.S. experiencing diagnosed episodes each year—but imagine how many other illnesses and ailments are caused by the disease? By hope-deprived living?"

"When something incredible like that happens to you, what do you do?"

"Well, I guess I'd say, 'Come check this out! Come and see!'" said Gus with enthusiasm that even surprised him.

"That's right! When you experience hope, real hope, you want to tell others. Come and see this!

"Think of those without fathers who need mentoring in hope and a bigger vision for life. Or what about all the leaders who quit leading because they've lost hope? Spiritual leaders. Teachers. CEOs. Think of the businesses that never get started, or the inventions that never get created, or the books that are never written. Think of the companies that struggle with underperforming or tuned-out employees. Think of broken marriages or divorces about to happen because one or the other in the relationship struggles with hope every day.

"I've experienced hope. Why keep that to myself?"

"I hear you."

"My dream is that this emotional and physical destroyer of life will be healed, but not with a new drug—by getting to the underlying issue…. We've lost sight of the way we were created to live. Live in hope! I want others to learn how to mentor and coach others to this kind of hope.

"Imagine if the poor were to seek education or meaningful employment because they discovered hope that their lives could make a difference? What if the rich and powerful saw this as a good thing and opened paths to education and meaningful employment to everyone? Would that be the Kingdom of God at hand?" Turnquest asked, now raising his voice as his own passion kicked in.

"Yeah, I guess it would," said Gus. "Sure, that would be something supernatural."

"Then let it begin with us. Let's do what it takes to live the Habits of Hope and share what we learn. Let's find those who've lost hope and come alongside them, not as their judges, but as those who invite them to the journey of a better way of life. A better way of leadership.

"Better period!"

Habit of Hope:

Empowering Others to Hope

Summarized: As you experience your own hope and find ways of defeating anxiety and depression, share your own story. Come alongside of those who've yet to live in hope and become a coach, mentor, or encourager for them to live into their destinies of hope and bigger purpose.

Realized: What benefit or benefits might you (and/or others) see or experience by you practicing the habit of *Empowering Others to Hope* as a way of life?

Evaluated: How far along are you in the *Empowering Others to Hope Habit* presently? (1 not at all to 10 completely)

1   2   3   4   5   6   7   8   9   10

Applied: What will you do to practice or grow the *Empowering Others to Hope Habit*?

Habit Releaser:

Create a list of those who need to learn and experience hope or, specifically these Habits of Hope. Who are they specifically or what kinds of people?

How might you see tangibly and purposefully coming alongside those who need to grow in hope?

Grab coffee or a meal with someone needing encouragement and hope with no other agenda but to be a friend and encourager.

Choose to meet regularly as a mentor or hope coach with someone for a period of time.

CHAPTER 27

PRACTICING HOPE

*"Action may not always bring happiness; but
there is no happiness without action."*

Benjamin Disraeli

After a short burst of rain, both men were amazed by a brilliant rainbow that appeared over Lake Hope. Gus grabbed his phone and took a picture as Turnquest stood mesmerized by its timing, as if there were a powerful meaning behind the rainbow.

"Things can change," said Mr. Turnquest. "The rainbow reminds me that God isn't done with making things new. Even what seems hopeless."

"Mr. T," said Gus, "that rainbow pretty much says it all! It's been an incredible time. I feel hopeful. You've not just encouraged me, but you've given me tools for the battle. Thank you."

"You're so welcome. But I've gotten a lot from sharing this with you, too. Trust me. Helping you helps my own soul.

"Would you like a cup of spring water, Gus?"

"Sure."

Mr. Turnquest walked over to an old, classic green hand pump and picked up a couple of glasses.

"Would you mind doing the honors?"

"Sure," said Gus, grabbing the handle and starting to pump. Again and again, Gus pumped the lever.

After a minute, no water had come out yet.

"Is the pump dry?"

"No. Just deep. Don't give up. Keep at it."

Finally, a few drops of water emerged from the spout—then more. Then almost without warning, huge gushes of cold, fresh well water poured out. Turnquest filled the glasses.

"Wow! That was harder work than I thought!" Gus exclaimed, still breathing hard.

"That's the Habits of Hope, right there. You start practicing a habit and you wonder whether you're making any progress—whether anything's changing. You wonder whether it's worth it. Then you start to notice a trickle. You feel happier. You're feeling excited about a day.

"Then here's the temptation. It's what most do. They quit just after seeing a bit of progress. They stop. Then, just like when the water falls all the way back to the bottom of the well, it's gonna take more to start over again.

"I've wondered about that. What keeps you from sinking back?"

"Over time, transformation becomes like gushing water. It's how positive habits work. With a little effort and consistency, hope keeps flowing and gains momentum. It then affects your work. Your health. Your relationships. Your spiritual life. And it builds on itself.

Fighting the Battle Each Day

"Gus, you referred to being given tools for the 'battle.' That is what you're fighting, you know. And with God's power, it's a winnable battle! The fight to live your purpose is a war—a winnable war, for sure, but still a war. And the payoff of meaning, peace of mind, and fulfillment can't be measured. It's priceless!

"I've always been a huge fan of great athletes, especially baseball players. My hero growing up was Joe DiMaggio. Incredible batter. Fifty-six-game hitting streak. His record still stands! My dad once asked me, 'Rodney, You wanna hit like Joe?' 'You bet!' I said. 'Then practice like Joe, Rodney. Study Joe. Swing like Joe. Go to batting cages.' And that's what's happens in Hope. We practice The Habits of Hope. And they've become us—second nature. They're in our fabric. But it all starts when you just do each Habit, one by one."

"I hear you," responded Gus. "And I've seen it in you and the people of Hope. They're charged up, no doubt!

Gus continued, "I'm wanting to make the Habits of Hope my way of life. I don't just want to know about them; I want to put them into practice! I want The Habits of Hope to become part of the fabric of my life. I need this to work and keep working!"

"I hear you," agreed Turnquest. "I felt that way when I first encountered the Habits. I wanted a magic pill for sure. But there are some really practical ways to make the Habits part of your day-to-day life. These things take The Habits of Hope from head to heart—to life. And I'm gonna challenge you to do them.

"First, just relax. It's okay to start implementing one, maybe two at a time. But do one each day.

"Second, you already understand that knowledge doesn't create power. The key is applied knowledge, applied wisdom. That's where the power lies!

"Practicing the Habits will unleash your bigger purpose. I guarantee it. But practice is key. Like learning a sport, an athlete practices the skills. One skill at a time. Live The Habits of Hope one day at a time—one Habit at a time. Living the Habits will unlock the purpose and life you've always wanted. Start with just one Habit and watch what happens, you'll realize the power and want all of them."

Cues to Remind Yourself

"The other key to unlock the power of The Habits of Hope is reminders, specific cues. Personally, I posted the list of The Habits of Hope on my mirror in the bathroom to remind me every single day. I'd encourage you to post them there or somewhere else you'll see them. Above your desk. In your car.

"As soon as you walk into the bathroom in the morning, you see the first cue. Think 'HEARING.' Then stop. Instead of starting your day with the usual onslaught of stuff to do, worries, or rush, remember and hear who you are: *I'm a blessed son.* 'I'm a child of God, not a slave to fear.' You may actually say it out loud. It works! You've got to try it!

"Then after grabbing a cup of coffee or tea or some water, go someplace you enjoy, a comfortable spot, and do some 'APPRECIATING.' Sit in a chair, maybe use a journal, or even your phone to start writing what you appreciate.

"Cues for BELIEVING can happen all day. But first and foremost, they happen when you read the Bible to start your day. Allow yourself to be captured by the fact that the God of the universe communicates and wants to be in touch with you. Why not allow the time and space for that communication?

"Other things can cue you to BELIEVING, too. When you see a beautiful lake, or field, or mountains, or even the sky, think, 'Wow! God's at work in the world!' When you come across someone with a need, that's a cue as well. How might God be at work in that person's need?

"I'd encourage you to find your cues. Where do you see God at work in the world?

And here, you'll want this," said Turnquest, holding out a small booklet in his hands.

"What's that?" asked Gus.

"It's 'The Habits of Hope Cheat Sheet. I put this together as a way for you to be reminded when you need to."

"That's awesome, Mr. T! I wrote a bunch of notes, but I still didn't want to forget what each habit was about!"

"Yeah, I realized that, so I created this a few years ago."

Become Part of a Group

"The SURROUNDING Habit empowers all of them. I'd encourage you to meet with some kind of positive group regularly or become part of a mentoring group or MasterMind. Talk about The Habits as part of your work. Maybe one each week or one a month, depending on how often you meet. Work your way through them, then cycle back.

"And Gus, there's no sacred or secular when it comes to these Habits. They're as relevant to business and health as they are to spiritual life. The Habits apply to all of life. Churches in Hope work through them. Also, apply them to business and watch how your business goes from being drudgery to being a powerful adventure!

"These habits affect your marriage. Do them with your wife or as part of a couples group.

Embrace Change and Transition

"Gus, I have a question for you: Do you think people like change?"

"Change? No, people don't like change. Do you think they do?" Gus asked.

"I do, yes. I think people actually like change," responded Turnquest to Gus' surprise.

"What? Really? You think people like change?"

"I do," Turnquest repeated. "I think most people want to change. They want a better life. More purpose. Progress. They want to be happier. Have better marriages. Lose the excess weight. Get more energy. Live their dreams."

"I'd agree with you on all that. But it seems like most shy away from change."

"Transition," Mr. Turnquest replied. "It's transition that's the problem. Transition's what keeps most people stuck. They don't know how to get from here to there. Or they don't know where to start. Or they're afraid they may take the risk and come back empty. Fail."

"I have a saying from Confucius written above my desk: '*A journey of a thousand miles begins with a single step.*' One step. Just one step. But just like walking, one step just naturally leads to another, and then you take the next one. Too many people just don't start."

"I agree. But why?" Gus asked.

Practice Hope by Killing Your Fears

"Because their fears control them. You can't fully launch your dreams or live out your purpose until you kill your fears. It's actually amazing how your fears begin to recede when you start taking action."

"Think of a public speaker. How would a person with fear of public speaking kill that fear?" Turnquest asked.

"Speak."

"You know it! You've probably heard that according to most studies, people's number one fear is public speaking. Number two is death. Death is number two! The comedian Jerry Seinfeld said, 'This means to the average person, if you go to a funeral, you're better off in the casket than doing the eulogy.'"

"That's hilarious!" Gus said, laughing.

"Fear keeps so many gifted people from using their gifts or living their purposes. Hope changes that!"

Mr. Turnquest then put his hand on Gus' chest and looked him in the eye.

"When you head home, I want to encourage you to just take one step. Something simple. Doable. What do you think?"

"I can do that," said Gus. "For me, the HEARING I'm blessed part's gotta be the starting point. When I see the first light each morning—for years, I've practiced telling myself I'm an idiot. I'm cursed. I stink. I've got to hear the voice of blessing, instead of cursing.

Practice Hope by Tracking Your Progress

Turnquest continued. "I also encourage you to find a way to track your progress. When you do each habit, just check off that you did it. One of the most powerful concepts that most humans fail to practice is the idea that we tend to attract what we track. When you want to save money, track your spending. When you want to start drinking ten glasses of water a day, check off every time you drink a glass. If you want to write your appreciation each day, track that you did it. When you want to live your purpose and become a person of Hope, track your Habits of Hope."

"How does someone do that, practically?" Gus asked. "How do you not become so busy that you lose track of things?"

"Simple. Keep a Habits of Hope list. You can write them in a journal or even track them on your phone with some kind of app that tracks habits. Track your food. Write down what you eat each day. Track your OFFERING. Just check it off when you've done something generous for someone. Get specific. Who was it? What did you do?

"This isn't rocket science. In the Bible, it says, 'A man reaps what he sows.' You just gotta decide:

"What do you want to reap?

"What outcome do you want?

"What will you do to sow?

"What are you gonna do each day to get there?

"And how will you know that you've done it?

"It's the eat the elephant one bite at a time thing again!

Practice Hope by Not Giving Up

"Just don't give up! And don't be disappointed when the seed you sow hasn't grown a huge bush and fruit over night! It's gonna take time. In that same passage, it says, 'Let's not become weary in doing good; for at the proper time, we will reap a harvest if we do not give up.'

"You know what that means in the original Greek, Gus?"

"What's that?"

"It means 'Don't give up!' Genius, huh? But the crazy thing about us humans is we're tempted to quit. We try a diet for a few days, then notice we didn't lose any weight. We quit. We quit things we join. We quit goals. We quit on our own dreams.

"Have you ever heard of Alexander Sportsoff?"

"No, I haven't," said Gus.

"Exactly! Because he quit! He gave up!" Turnquest said, proudly smiling at his own humor. "God hasn't given you a spirit of timidity. God gave you a spirit of power and love and self-discipline. It's what God's like! It's what God does! God empowers us. But when you get moving, then watch what God does!

"As you practice the Habits of Hope, they'll become you. And even more importantly, God will empower you and breathe life into you and through you. And just like that, you have cold well water flowing from the pump. You start creating the momentum of Hope every single day," Turnquest said.

Habit Releaser for Practicing Hope

Print and post a list of The Habits of Hope and put them somewhere you'll see them each day.

Remember you don't need to grow all Habits at once. Pick one or two to start with and track those.

Create or join a group to go through the Habits of Hope. Discuss one habit a week and hold each other accountable to apply them. Share your successes and setbacks.

CHAPTER 28

GOING HOME—A SECOND CHANCE

"For I know the plans I have for you," declares the Lord, "plans to prosper you and not to harm you, plans to give you hope and a future."

— Jeremiah 29:11-13

W hen Gus said goodbye to Mr. Turnquest early the next morning, it surprisingly felt like one of the most difficult goodbyes he had ever experienced. This whole wild trip had been a surprise. But as he looked at the man who'd saved his life, he felt like he was looking into the eyes of pure love.

"Will I see you again?" Gus asked.

"I sure hope so!" said Turnquest. "I want you to know—I believe in you. You're okay. You're really okay. Frankly, I love you, Partner."

Again, tears welled up in Gus' eyes. It was a whole new experience to him—having so seldom heard those words made them land somewhere deep inside his soul. The words "I love you" seemed to have more weight because they were coming from another man who wasn't his biological father. Yet in many ways, that's exactly what Rodney Turnquest was to Gus. A father. A real father.

In a world where most men are so fatherless in many ways, Gus felt love from another man in the purest of ways—a life-changing way.

Gus looked out at the lake one more time and saw the view he had also received as a gift—the mountains. He felt gratitude for that. Then he embraced Rodney Turnquest.

"Thank you! Thank you!"

Gus slid into the driver's seat and waved as he headed up the Turnquest driveway. He looked in his rearview mirror and once more glimpsed the man he'd known since he was a child. Gus honked his horn as if in tribute for a life well-lived—a job well-done.

Heading Home

As Gus left Hope and headed out on Route 8 toward the New York Thruway, his mind buzzed with all he'd experienced over the last few days. As he drove, he looked in his rearview mirror and was surprised to see a glow around Hope. It was beautiful. Mesmerizing. So much so that Gus didn't even notice a fast-moving greenish storm approaching.

With what seemed like no notice at all, Gus's car was hit with a barrage of pelting rain, hail stones, and the whizz of branches. The unusually powerful and sudden storm blinded Gus as he tried to react to the instant change. He turned his wipers to high, trying to see, but to no effect. Gus was blinded.

Realizing he needed to pull off the road, he quickly aimed for the side of the road, but at that same moment, another car came at him head on, horn blaring, and headlights blinding. Gus knew instantly that doing nothing wasn't an option.

Gus jerked the wheel left to avoid the car, and with no chance to correct, skidded off the road, through a row of small trees, and into Lake Hope. With the airbags failing to inflate, Gus smacked his head on the window as he was jerked sideways while the car spun out of control and plunged into the lake. Only partially conscious, Gus found himself soaking wet and immersed in cold water rising all around him.

"Oh God, this isn't good," he thought. He felt blood oozing from his head and the jolt of cold water all around him. He had a strange sense of just wanting to go to sleep. Then some other voice kicked in. "Get out of this car. Just keep going. You can't give up," he urged himself on. "You can make it! This doesn't have to be the end! Live, Gus! Live! Live!"

Gus forced himself through the broken window and swam with all his might as rain continued pelting him. He found the shore.

A mix of blood and water dripped from Gus's head. At first, he didn't remember where he was or how'd he gotten there. Images of a canoe entered his mind. He was confused as he curled up in the tall grass on the side of the lake.

Discovered

It was some time later when Sheriff Pete Sidney happened by and saw a car in a ditch on the side of the road. The driver was still in the car, clearly shaken, but okay. After helping the driver, the sheriff noticed some small trees knocked over on the other side of the road. Sidney struggled through the tangled brush toward the lake. He pulled up short when he saw the car's trunk sticking out of the water. As he rushed to see whether the car was occupied, he tripped over the body of Gus Thompson.

Pete noticed a huge gash and dried blood on the man's head and face. As he bent down, fully expecting the man to be lifeless, Gus rolled over and gasped. The typically professional sheriff jumped back in an instant, as if he'd just experienced his own version of a zombie apocalypse.

"Whoa, my God! You're alive!"

Pete knew not to move the victim, so he covered him in a blanket and told him help was on the way. He called for an ambulance, which arrived quickly and whisked Gus off to St. Luke's Hospital in Utica. He had Gus's car extracted from the lake and brought down to Utica as well.

Gus spent the next few days in the hospital being scanned, poked, and prodded. Police and hospital staff tried to contact his family but had no luck. For some reason, Amy's phone went right to voicemail. Gus was on his own.

The whack on Gus's head was his most concerning injury, but within a few days, Gus was fit enough to leave the hospital. Reluctantly, his doctor released him on his own. Gus made his way to Jack's Body and Brakes where his scratched and dented car waited.

With his car in working condition, although smelling a bit like fish, Gus decided not to call Amy and alarm her—or make her feel like she had to drive all the way to Western New York to get him.

Heading Home Again

As Gus got into the car to start his drive back home, he actually felt pretty good, even rested from his stay in the hospital. It was at this point that memories started to come flooding back to him. Why he had driven up to the Adirondacks in the first place. Rodney Turnquest. Hope. The Habits of Hope. The weird aura around Hope before the sudden accident.

"Oh my gosh!" thought Gus. "Was this whole thing a dream? Mr. Turnquest. The way of life in Hope? The Habits of Hope?"

Yet, Gus couldn't deny the sense of peace he felt. Was it the whack on the head? The medication he had been given? No. It couldn't be. Hope really happened! He could feel it!

Typically when driving, Gus tended to put on either talk radio or switch between music channels. This time, the silence seemed soothing. The road felt smooth and the sky looked bluer than it had in a long time. He noticed the cows on the side of the road. The orchards. The fields being harvested.

As Gus drove, it felt like he was leaving behind his own sorrow and memories of what life *hadn't* been for too many years.

It was almost as if the magic of the mountains had reinforced the hope that there was good in life, maybe a lot of good Gus had been missing for years—too many years.

In all of his struggles to make a living, Gus missed the memo that job number one was to make a life. A good life. To discover and engage his own purpose.

But after his encounter in Hope, it was as if Gus were coming home to some place totally new. He felt he'd been set free and was about to walk into doors he'd never imagined opening, or at least opening for him.

The mountains were part of his healing. That's something mountains have the power to do. And they weren't the only part—there was also the loving wisdom of a mentor who believed in him. Add an example of someone else who'd moved from living in his own private hell to experiencing the power of Hope.

Gus had a new understanding of a way of life that was both grounded in ancient wisdom and practical and actionable in the here and now. It was the real remedy for what ailed him. No pill could offer this kind of cure. And Gus now knew that what really ailed him was his own soul's unsettled lack of direction.

The road went on for many miles, heading west past Buffalo, then through downtown Cleveland, and through the many miles stretching across Ohio and Indiana.

Gus enjoyed the ride. It was as if his typically angry, frustrated, or preoccupied brain was able to settle into the rhythm of the highway. The passing miles didn't feel hard like other trips had in the past.

Arriving Again

When at last Gus pulled into his driveway, he wondered, "How will I explain what's happened to Amy? *Can* I explain this to Amy?" He took a deep breath, opened the car door, and walked in the back door of the house. All that came to mind was Vivien Leigh's final words in *Gone With the Wind*, "Tomorrow is another day."

"Gus!" Amy shrieked, seeing him walk in through the laundry room door. "Where have you been? We've all been worried about you! How did you drive yourself home? I thought you were in a hospital! What in the world happened to you?"

"Dad! What are you doing home?" asked his son Ben with more concern than he'd shared in a while.

"What do you mean?" said Gus, startled by their responses. "I didn't want you to worry. I guess I should have called before driving home."

"We got messages saying you were in an accident. There were a bunch of voicemails trying to get a hold of me and this stupid cell phone just got them to me when we got back from Mom's. The doctor said you'd been hurt! They found you semi-conscious on the side of a lake in the mountains. We were just getting ready to either drive or fly to New York."

"Good you didn't," said Gus.

"We were shocked when we got those messages. My cell phone was dead all weekend. I had no idea! I just got the messages. Are you okay?"

"No. I mean yes. I'm okay. I'm fine! I'd say. Just a big scrape on my head. I guess I hit it pretty hard."

"I was really scared when I got those messages, Gus."

"You were?" Gus was confused and at the same time touched by Amy's clear outpouring of concern and gratitude that he was okay.

"Where were you, Gus? I had no idea where you were. So when I got those voicemails from a hospital from Utica, I couldn't figure out why you were there in the first place. Last I knew, you were in Cleveland."

"Well," said Gus, still shaken, "actually, I was in Cleveland. But I took a trip to the Adirondacks. I was in Hope over the last few days. Amy, I don't even know how to begin to describe what I've just been through. Yeah, I was in some kind of accident. And I think I almost drowned. Well, I mean I was drowning," Gus said, somewhat puzzled by his own words.

Amy squinted at him. Confused. Gus had seen this look before. He'd seen it when he came home late and said it was because he'd been working and got stuck in traffic. It meant she was wondering whether to believe him.

"Amy, I went to Hope after getting a letter a few months back from a guy I knew growing up, Rodney Turnquest. I just had the most incredible experience of my life in Hope. I feel like someone just took a scalpel, opened up my soul, and put something new inside me. Maybe something I've never had before. Or if I did, I lost it a long, long time ago!"

As he said this, tears welled up in his eyes. "Amy. I don't know where to start. Well, actually I do. Amy, I'm sorry. I am so, so sorry. I've been an absolute jerk. All I can say is I'm sorry. I'm really sorry."

Again, Amy gave him a confused look, not even knowing whether the whack on his head had done some damage. Too many times she'd tried to hold out hope that this time it would be different. "I'm sorry" didn't seem to mean much to Gus. Common words from his mouth but nothing changed. And if there's such a thing as "hope-fatigue," Amy had it.

Sure the whole accident thing had shaken her up, and the fact that she was worried, then happy that Gus was okay made her realize he still held some place of love in her heart. But it had been years since she'd seen tears like this in Gus's eyes. And the way Gus spoke was far from typical.

"Gus," she said, "I so want to believe you. I do. Honestly, I see something in your eyes that's not what I usually see. I'm glad you're OK. But there's been a lot of water under the bridge. Sorry for what? You've told me you're sorry a lot, and Gus, things just never change.

"You know I'd love things to be different. But it's just too hard for me to hold on to hope that's the case. I've been there, done that. I'm glad for you, Gus. But I'm just not ready to go there."

Gus opened his mouth to start sharing why everything was going to be different now. This was all something new. Then he stopped. He noticed he felt defensive and stopped himself from giving into his instinctive response. In the past, he would have reflexively tried to convince Amy she was wrong. He'd start telling her all about

Rodney Turnquest. He'd tell her about The Habits of Hope. He wanted to tell her about the letter, the vision Turnquest had shared, the destiny the people of Hope saw in him, and the power of his gifts.

But he stopped. This wasn't usual for Gus.

Gus realized the proof would be in actions, not words. For the first time in a long time, he felt he finally had the tools that would lead to the change he really wanted. He possessed a path and practical actions he could take to move forward. To live in Hope instead of helplessness—purpose instead of futility. And Gus believed he didn't need to prove it to anyone.

"Amy, I totally understand why you'd feel that way. Totally get it! I've given you plenty of evidence over the years that I don't always do what I say I'm going to do. I've given you plenty of 'This time it will be different' speeches. And all I can say, as inadequate as this may sound, is I'm sorry. I'm really, really sorry. I understand it will take a long time to earn your trust back—if I even can."

Then Gus did another thing he hadn't done in a long time. He left it at that. He didn't try to prove anything. He didn't even ask her to listen to his whole story—all about Hope and the Habits and how it could bring change—nothing. He just left it at "I'm sorry" and "I know I must work hard to regain your trust."

Amy nodded. Again, she recalled the relief, the joy, of seeing him alive and well. Yet she also knew she'd put her heart out there way too many times to accept this was something different. All she could do was stare at the man she had loved enough to marry and nod. Just nod.

"Amy, I'm really glad to be home. I've got a lot of work to do. I get it. And for the first time in a long time, I'm excited about that. I'm really excited about it. I'm glad to be alive. Or still alive. Or whatever I am!"

"I guess so!" said Amy with the hint of a smile. "Yeah, I guess you have some explaining to do."

"Sure do, don't I?"

POSTSCRIPT

"Those who keep speaking about the sun while walking under a cloudy sky are messengers of hope, the true saints of our day."

— Henri Nouwen

For years, Gus wondered why every effort to contact Rodney Turnquest, or the others he had met in Hope, was fruitless. He tried searching the Internet for information on Turnquest, or on the incredible transformation in Hope, but to no avail. He started to think maybe he really had dreamed this whole thing while he was laid up in the hospital. Had he?

Yet there was no getting around other facts: As Gus leaned in to practicing the Habits of Hope, his life changed. His relationships changed. Significantly, he found himself actively going about his life according to his bigger purpose.

Gus did everything Turnquest shared with him, including posting a copy of the Habits of Hope in his room and office. Real progress took place. Unlike other self-growth approaches he had tried, or even pills he had taken, the Habits of Hope didn't wear off or become outdated.

Gus never again fell deep into depression, experienced chronic anxiety, desperation, or a lack of direction. Instead, the Habits of Hope became a daily way of life—a pattern that could be repeated day after day and week after week.

The results of The Habits of Hope compound over time until there is a snowball of powerful effects, both internally and externally, as things change. Like a penny doubled every day, at first the results seemed minor. Just sixteen cents in five days. Five dollars and twelve cents after ten days. Even after twenty days, the results are only $52.43. But after thirty days, that magic penny becomes over 5 million dollars. And the next day, at thirty-one days, the penny would be worth over 10.7 million dollars!

Though most people possess lottery-like wishful thinking that things change just because they want them to, it doesn't usually work that way. Lasting, purposeful, and holistic change and life success happen one day at time. Gus realized what many accomplished athletes or musicians know. Practice and hard work pay off over time. Living by The Habits of Hope has guaranteed outcomes, just not instant outcomes.

At first, Amy would view Gus' new habits and practices with suspicion. She would notice words like *"hearing"* posted on the bathroom mirror. She would notice Gus getting up a bit earlier and making lists of things he appreciated. She would see him meeting online with what he called his "MasterMind" group on Tuesday afternoons. She would notice Gus drinking more water, watching his diet, and getting to bed earlier each night. But most surprising of all, Amy would appreciate the way Gus encouraged her to invest in her own life—his "go for it" attitude when it came to her own dreams and desires.

Something was different.

As Gus continued to practice these habits, day in and day out—just a few habits at a time—things started to change. First in Gus, then in a continual snowball of powerful effects, influence, and even income. Then, as others began to see a kind of happiness, peace, and vision in Gus, they started to ask, "What are you up to? How did you become an overnight success?"

Gus would laugh when others spoke of him as an overnight success. He chuckled at the thought that they saw him as a success at all. And when others asked him how to create the kind of passionate marriage he and Amy shared, he was even more shocked. And he would think, "If they only knew!"

Over time, even Amy began to encourage Gus to share what he'd learned about Hope and The Habits of Hope. And slowly, in small groups, he would share his story and the concept of The Habits of Hope. Men's groups. Women's groups. Entrepreneur groups. Church groups. Corporate leader groups. Gus shared with them all over time.

Some scoffed and laughed at Gus' story and wondered whether he had been drunk that October weekend. Others just thought he had some bizarre dream when he was in the hospital. But over time, more and more people became interested and wanted to hear the story of Hope from Gus's perspective. Maybe it did exist! Then a few actually came to Gus later and asked, "Gus, would you share with me more about these Habits of Hope and how I might be able to apply them in my situation?"

As more and more men and women began to practice The Habits of Hope, talk about them, and find ways to track their progress, things began to change. More people began loving their work and new companies started. Rates of depression in certain areas decreased. Suicide rates dropped to almost none where Gus lived. Creativity, business growth, and entrepreneurship began to increase. New educational strategies and new spiritual communities, groups, and churches began to flourish, first in the region, then emanating from there.

Places where hope had been absent became places of restored hope. Families began to experience the joy of being families with a bigger purpose. Companies became communities of vision that saw themselves as conduits to transform lives and create human flourishing in a world where God was at work.

Gus continued trying to get in touch with Rodney Turnquest but to no avail. It was almost as if he had disappeared.

"URGENT!"

All that changed early one autumn afternoon, Gus received a text message with the words: "URGENT: Gus, there's been an accident up in Hope and my dad is in serious condition. He is asking to see you. Doctors don't think he has long. Would you come to see him at the Nathan Littauer Hospital in Gloversville?" The message was signed "Sarah Lowell."

Gus didn't recognize the number, and at first, he was tempted to ignore it, thinking it was sent to him by mistake. "That name is familiar, though," Gus thought as he ran through the neighborhood trails as he now did religiously. "Sarah Lowell.... Wait! That's Rodney Turnquest's daughter," he suddenly remembered.

Gus took the short way home and reread the message. Then his heart began to race and tears poured from his eyes. The man who had transformed his life was alive and was in trouble. And Gus would do anything for him. Even his own tears reminded him how much Mr. Turnquest had changed his life. There was a time when nothing touched Gus in an emotional way. But the love and gratitude he felt for this man, this mentor....

Gus cancelled everything he had going on that day, called Amy, and told her what had happened. At Amy's insistence, she joined him as together they made the journey to upstate New York.

As Gus drove, he realized his life-changing trip to Hope had been exactly ten years prior. Once again, as he drove with his wife, he was overwhelmed with the remarkable color and feel of the Adirondacks clothed in their best dress. Amy and Gus held hands as they drove, and Gus pointed out key landmarks along the route that meant so much to him.

Seeing Mr. T for the Last Time

Gus and Amy headed straight to the hospital in Gloversville, where Sarah told Gus her father had been taken. After checking with the desk, Gus and Amy were directed to the intensive care unit on the second floor.

When the two walked into the room, Rodney's daughter, Sarah Lowell, greeted both of them, and after introducing herself to them, she told them, "My father had surgery early this morning. The doctors are in there now checking his vitals. They should be out soon. We can sit in this room down the hall until we can go in."

The three sat down, and Sarah shared that her dad had been mountain biking on trails with a friend. "Crazy, right? Ageless, my dad! He was going down a hill and popped a tire. He came off the bike and hit a tree, fracturing several ribs and hitting his head. The doctors are concerned about internal bleeding and blood clots at this point. It's pretty uncertain."

"How old is your dad, anyway?" asked Gus.

"Well..." paused Sarah, almost uncertain how to answer. "In Hope years, my dad's only middle-aged. People in Hope don't live forever. They just live longer and better than the rest of the world."

"So, Hope is a real place then?" asked Amy.

"A real place?" questioned Sarah. "Well, Hope's more real than other places. So real, most of us never want to leave."

"You can go in now," said a tall, middle-aged nurse.

The three walked toward the door and into the room. "Mr. T?" said Gus gently.

"Hey, Gus, is that you?" said a voice from behind the curtain.

"Yes, Mr. Turnquest, I'm here. And I brought Amy."

"Hi, Amy. I've heard a lot about you," he said, between intermittent gasps of breath, as Gus and Amy stepped around the curtain. "Thank you for coming, Gus. Amy, you're a blessed woman. Gus is quite a man."

"Yes, I know," said Amy. "I know you are too, Mr. Turnquest"

"Mr. T, I'm so sorry for your accident," said Gus.

"Ah, Gus, all part of the great adventure. But I'm not doing so great, they tell me. I asked Sarah to tell you to come because I want to share something with you, and I wasn't sure how much time I have left. Gus, it's about the words on my headstone. Do you remember them?"

"I remember you showed them to me—from Dostoevsky?"

'For the secret of man's being is not only to live...but to live for something definite. Without a firm notion of what he is living for, man will not accept life and will rather destroy himself than remain on earth....'

"I will die empty," said Mr. Turnquest. "I've lived for something definite. And I will die empty."

"What? What do you mean by 'die empty'?"

"It's a good thing. It's how everybody should die! It means I've finished my mission. I've done what I'm supposed to in the world. Actually, there's just one more thing I need to do, and that's why I had you come.

"Even if I don't get many more days, I've finished what I was born to do. Most won't get that privilege, mostly because they don't know how to live in consistent hope. They don't know about having a vision for their lives that's bigger than them, or having mentors that help them discover and engage their purpose. It's time for people to live for something definite. We were created for that purpose. We were meant to die empty, having fulfilled our destinies, our bigger purpose. But without The Habits of Hope, most won't and can't. So I have come here from Hope to do my last job.

"What job is that Mr. T?" asked Gus, as Amy looked on with tears streaming down her face.

"My last job is to pass the baton—pass the baton of this message of Hope to you.

"Gus, the reason I felt it was so important to see you one last time was because of another dream I had. I dreamed I went to a funeral and saw an open casket. When I approached the casket, I saw a runner in the casket, fully dressed in running clothes. But it was the saddest thing. Something was wrong. Even sadder than death. The runner still had a baton in his hand. It was weird. Like he had run his race, but he hadn't passed his baton before he died."

"What did that mean to you, Mr. T?"

"It meant he died without giving his greatest gift! It was a tragedy. Do you see? Relay runners fail if they never pass the baton. If they don't entrust someone else with leadership, they lose the race, even if they've run a good one. We're all meant to pass our baton to someone else. People who don't or won't pass the baton fail. The vision and the wisdom dies with them. It's why the world is still such a mess. That can change, Gus. Do you see that? Do you see it?"

"I do. And I'm forever grateful you saw it too, Mr. T."

"I'm passing the baton of The Habits of Hope dream to you. I've carried the vision of Hope for the last fifty years. Will you share this? Teach it? Coach others? Will you equip others outside of Hope to live in HOPE? Will you entrust others who will then mentor and coach others?"

"There's nothing I'd rather give my life for. And I've been doing that since you taught me. I accept the baton."

Mr. Turnquest looked up at Gus from his hospital bed, tubes in his arms and nose, tears in his eyes and on his bruised cheeks.

"Thank you, Gus. Thank you."

"I can attest to that—he'll do it, Mr. Turnquest," said Amy. "He's already doing it. Gus is a different man since he found how to live in Hope. I'm different. We're different. And I now share The Habits with others as well. Our sons do, too."

"Mr. Turnquest, so Hope is a real place then, isn't it?" asked Amy.

"More real than any other place," said Mr. Turnquest.

"It doesn't take many to bring this revolution of Hope to the world. Just a handful of people who really practice Hope authentically and intentionally. You came to Hope that fall for bigger reasons than you can know. Much bigger," Mr. Turnquest said softly.

"Yes, sir. I know it and I get it now. I know what my mission is."

"Good. I always knew you were a good man. Do me proud. I know you will. You are blessed," Turnquest said.

"Hey, Mr. T, did they ever figure out who was the guy who drowned in the lake the day I showed up in Hope?"

"Yeah, they did. His name was Gus Thompson."

"What? It was me?"

"Yeah. He died. But because he died many, many others came to life.

"Haha!" Mr. Turnquest chuckled out loud. "It's been taught, 'Unless a kernel of wheat falls to the ground and dies, it remains only a single seed. But if it dies, it produces many seeds.' Gus, more has come from that guy drowning than you can imagine."

Then, without warning, Mr. Turnquest's head slumped back and his breathing stopped. The monitors beeped loudly and his pulse flat-lined.

The room quickly became a blur of doctors, nurses, lights, and machines. Yet Gus knew Rodney Turnquest's time was done, and he couldn't have been more at peace about what was happening.

"Unless a kernel of wheat falls to the ground and dies," Gus said out loud. There couldn't have been a more fitting exit for a man whose life had been about instilling real life into others.

Rodney Turnquest had finished his race. He had kept the faith. He had passed the baton.

"You lived for something definite, Mr. T. Now it's our turn…" said Gus. "Well done."

THE HABITS OF HOPE

HEARING: Hearing You Are Blessed

APPRECIATING: Appreciating the Good

BELIEVING: Believing God is at Work and Joining Him

INVESTING: Investing in Yourself and Your Dreams

TRUSTING: Trusting God's Rhythms

SURROUNDING: Surrounding Yourself with Positive People

OFFERING: Offering Your Gifts Generously

FUELING: Fueling Your Brain

HYDRATING: Hydrating Your Body Continuously

OVERCOMING: Overcoming Setbacks Constantly

PROGRESSING: Progressing Toward Your Vision Daily

EMPOWERING: Empowering Others to Hope

THE HABITS OF HOPE
CHEAT SHEET

HEARING: Hearing You Are Blessed

Defeat the voices of fear and cursing that want to ruin every good thing. Intentionally tune in to the truth of your real identity as one who is loved, blessed, and courageous.

APPRECIATING: Appreciating the Good

Intentionally change your focus from fearful and damaging thoughts by replacing those with all that is good. Change your brain! Find things in your life and surroundings to be grateful for and actively note them in lists of appreciation.

BELIEVING: Believing God Is at Work and Joining Him

Practice looking for places and ways God is at work building His Kingdom all around you in the world. See yourself as involved in

God's bigger purpose and let that create in you deep enjoyment and significance for the work you do every day. A clarity and a confidence.

INVESTING: Investing in Yourself and Your Dreams

Realize who you really are, what you desire, and what you have to offer. Then invest in your growth and dreams to help you become that real you. Stay motivated by a positive picture of you in the future. Invest money, time, and resources to best succeed in doing what you do best.

TRUSTING: Trusting God's Rhythms

Trust in God's unforced rhythms in the world and experience "kairos" by intentionally taking breaks from your work or whatever you feel compelled to do periodically. Allow yourself to fully enjoy each moment and be okay with things not all being perfect or realized yet. Let go of the need to be in control of all the outcomes.

SURROUNDING: Surrounding Yourself with Positive People

Find other hopeful or positive people who become part of a group who won't let each other settle for mediocrity or negativity. Join or create positive or MasterMind groups where together you do more than any one of you could do isolated or alone.

OFFERING: Offering Your Gifts Generously

Intentionally experience and express the convergence of your passions, proficiencies, and platform to utilize those. Educate and excavate your gifts; then be a good steward of those as you use them to benefit other people and enjoy the fulfillment and freedom that comes by offering your authentic gifts out of joy and generosity.

FUELING: Fueling Your Brain

Maintain and grow the health and wellbeing of your brain as a regular priority. Your brain's physical health is key to your hope and fulfilling your bigger purpose. Fuel your brain with regular movement, restful practices, and peaceful sleep. Eat food that enables your brain to work at maximum capacity.

HYDRATING: Hydrating Your Body Continuously

Hydrate your body with water continually and watch how other things become easier for you. Drink water as soon as you get up each morning and regularly throughout the day.

OVERCOMING: Overcoming Setbacks Constantly

Since adversity is part of life, choose to grow and persevere and even gain experience and expertise through it. Overcoming your setbacks is your personal courageous choice. Expect adversity and counter it with resilience, faith, and hope to overcome your setbacks and continue living into your bigger purpose.

PROGRESSING: Progressing Toward Your Vision Daily

Gain clarity of your vision and take small steps regularly to move in that direction each day. Don't worry about doing too much at once. Instead, ask yourself regular questions to gain clarity on what's most important and must be done each day to move a little bit further in the right direction.

EMPOWERING: Empowering Others to Hope

As you experience your own hope and find ways of defeating anxiety and depression, share your own story. Come alongside of those who've yet to live in hope and become a coach, mentor, or encourager for them to live into their destinies of hope and bigger purpose.

About the Author

Jeff Caliguire is an author, professional keynote speaker, leadership and purpose coach, wealth advisor, and entrepreneur. He lives firmly by his mission to "unlock people to discover, engage, and invest in their callings and dreams, one person at a time."

After experiencing seasons of depression and dissatisfaction, Jeff became convinced there had to be a better form of education beyond traditional degrees. It involved the deeper education of the soul and the intentional extraction of one's God-given gifts, passions, and deeper purpose for work, leadership, and life.

After mentoring from Bobb Biehl and Ralph Mattson, Jeff discovered his gifts and his passion, both centered around helping others discover and engage their real God-given potential. After working with Ralph Mattson to host Leadership Refineries in the late 1990s, Jeff began studying life, career, and leadership coaching by taking courses from the "father of modern life coaching," Thomas Leonard and his organization, Coach U.

After serving as senior pastor of Beacon Community Church, president of Operation Beacon Street, and founding the Boston Sports Fellowship in 2001, Jeff began coaching professionally and leading retreats for leaders and organizations. He then authored *Leadership Secrets of Saint Paul* (River Oak Publishing, 2003), co-authored *Shifting Into Higher Gear: An Owner's Manual for Uniting Your Calling and Career* with Tom Siciliano (Josse Bass, 2005), and wrote *Unlocking Your Convergence Point: 7 Keys to Freeing the*

Work You Were Born to Do (Convergence Point, 2016). He also writes regularly on self-leadership, career, entrepreneurship, and practical spirituality at JeffCaliguire.com.

In 2015, Jeff worked with his close friend and college roommate, Gregg Stutts, to found and build a network called, "Entrepreneur on Purpose." Jeff and Gregg lead MasterMind groups and retreats, and they host a weekly podcast called, "Entrepreneur on Purpose." It can be found on iTunes or at www.EOPurpose.com.

Jeff speaks to leaders, men's groups, churches, and businesses on the topic of integrating practical self-leadership habits into life, as well as topics covered in his other books.

Originally from Northern New Jersey, Jeff spends his summers and as many winter weekends as possible in the Adirondacks in upstate New York. He attended Cornell University, where he received a BA in government, played football, and met and married his college sweetheart, Mindy.

The Caliguires then moved to Dallas, Texas, where Jeff received a Master's in Theology from Dallas Theological Seminary. Jeff has also worked in the financial industry in wealth management with Smith Barney, and he currently serves clients and owns his own firm, Convergence Point Wealth Advisors. (www.CPWAdvisors.com)

Since he was a small child, Jeff has not missed spending time each summer in the Adirondacks, in particular, Speculator, New York. Jeff and Mindy have three sons, Jeff, Jon, and Josh, and currently make their home in Boulder, Colorado, where Jeff hikes in the foothills of the Rockies with his dogs or whoever else will join him.

About Convergence Point Coaching

Convergence Point was founded in 2008, with a vision of empowering individuals and businesses that were ready to "unlock their unique purpose and potential."

Using our state of the art, proprietary tools and programs, we coach you to:

1. **Maximize your motivated strengths and abilities.** (This clearly starts by knowing them with clarity.)

2. **Minimize what holds you back.** (This includes knowing how to defeat all fear and move forward with confidence.)

3. **Multiply daily wins in order to achieve your goals and desires.** (This includes being able to set and complete short- and long-term goals and objectives.)

Contact us if you're interested in making the "big shift" to moving your life, livelihood, or leadership to a whole new level of influence, while continually advancing hope! We can work with you in person (if geographically possible), virtually, or in one-, two-, or three-day retreats. We can also include spouses or partners in the retreats.

For a thirty-minute, complimentary Big Shift Consultation, contact us at:

www.Convergencepoint.Biz
Jeff.Caliguire@ConvergencePoint.biz
(224) 232-7126

About Convergence Point Wealth Advisors

Since 2008, Convergence Point Wealth Advisors has been helping people ensure their money serves them and empowers them to fulfill their God-given purpose and potential.

If you resonate with the concepts of this book, we would like to help empower you to live your dream, fund your future priorities, and align with your most important values...what we call "Managing Money on Purpose."

The difference between us and most traditional or transactional financial services is our relational and holistic approach: We begin with you and your life vision and then help you clearly align your money and other financial resources to turn your dream into reality. We work hard to help you get there and then stay focused to continue in that direction.

The two primary outcomes we seek for our clients are:

1. **Clarity:** You know where you're going and how you will get there.

2. **Confidence:** You feel great about decisions you've made in light of economic and personal realities.

And when you have clarity and confidence in financial issues, you also enjoy peace of mind. Whether you're managing a fortune worth many millions or the small fortune that paying for a college education requires, your plan and purposeful wealth management should serve you and your dream. We understand that!

With this in mind, we encourage our clients to begin with what we call Financial Life Planning.

Then when ready, we offer a select array of financial products and opportunities to support your plan, including:

- 401k Rollovers (when you leave a company/retire)
- Separately Managed Accounts
- Principal Protection Strategies and ETFs
- Corporate Retirement Plans
- Online Access to Accounts
- IRAs
- Annuities
- Conservative Investment Strategies
- Check a Month for Current Income
- Tax Sensitive Accounts

For a complimentary "Money on Purpose Consultation," email Jeff. Caliguire@CPWAdvisors or call 224-232-7126.

About Entrepreneur on Purpose

Entrepreneur on Purpose exists to empower those with a vision or God-sized dreams to become part of a larger community and gain the resources to "kill your fears and launch your dreams."

We host a regular podcast as well as training through forums, seminars, and MasterMind groups to empower you to fulfill your God-given potential while experiencing the adventure, fun, and joy that comes when you use your best gifts, resources, and talents.

The best ways to get involved with Entrepreneur on Purpose include:

- Facebook Group: Go to "Entrepreneur on Purpose Community" and ask to join.

- Podcast: You can access the "Entrepreneur on Purpose" podcast on iTunes or at EntrepreneuronPurpose.Libsyn. com.

- Website: www.EOPurpose.com, which includes blog, resources, and training

Book Jeff Caliguire to Speak at Your Next Event

Jeff Caliguire is an author, professional keynote speaker, leadership and business coach, wealth advisor, and entrepreneur. As the President of Convergence Point, Convergence Point Wealth Advisors, and co-founder of Entrepreneur on Purpose, he helps people unlock their purposes and build purpose-focused businesses, teams, and lives.

Jeff has been coaching and leading retreats professionally for more than fifteen years. He is available to speak to any group or any organization, no matter what size. He will personally tailor his speech or presentation to fit your audience and its needs.

To find out what value Jeff can bring to your organization and to arrange a complimentary 30-minute interview, contact Jeff at:

Jeff.Caliguire@ConvergencePoint.biz

(224) 232-7126